THE FOUNDATIONS OF EDUCATION SERIES

Understanding Children of Poverty

DAVID GOTTLIEB
Job Corps, Office of Economic Opportunity

CHARLES E. RAMSEY
University of Minnesota

Series Editor
JUDSON T. SHAPLIN
Graduate Institute of Education
Washington University, St. Louis

Science Research Associates, Inc.   Chicago

A Subsidiary of IBM

Library of Congress Catalog Card Number: 67-25035

Acknowledgments

The editors and the publisher wish to express their gratitude for the courtesy and cooperation shown by the many authors, literary agents, and publishers who were kind enough to grant permission for the use of the selections in this volume.

AMERICAN PSYCHOLOGICAL ASSOCIATION. P. 70: From "Review of Evidence Relating to Effects of Desegregation on the Intellectual Performance of Negroes," by Irwin Katz, as it appeared in the *American Psychologist* Magazine, Vol. XIX (June 1964).

AMERICAN SOCIOLOGICAL ASSOCIATION. P. 54: From "Teaching and Students: The Views of Negro and White Teachers," by David Gottlieb, as it appeared in *Sociology of Education*, Vol. XXXVII (Summer 1964).

COMMISSION ON COMMUNITY RELATIONS OF THE CITY OF DETROIT, MICHIGAN. P. 54: From "The Challenge to Education in the Multi-Problem Neighborhoods," a mimeographed report prepared by the Research Committee of the Coordinating Council on Human Relations of Detroit, April 20, 1961.

FREE PRESS (a subsidiary of Crowell Collier & Macmillan, Inc.). P. 48: From *The Adolescent Society*, by James S. Coleman. © The Free Press, a Corporation, 1961.

This book is dedicated to the many thousands of young men and women who have become part of the Job Corps. By your presence and your participation, you have made it abundantly clear that poor youth have both the desire and the ability to become people of dignity — eager for involvement in our society.

Preface

The primary aim of the FOUNDATIONS OF EDUCATION SERIES is to apply current research and theory in the behavioral and social sciences to the study of American education. The series will provide students, teachers, school administrators, and other educators with illuminating examples of how and why sociologists, anthropologists, political scientists, economists, and social psychologists are contributing new directions and new vitality to the system and the process of education. Each book in the series is an original work by an author who in his own research, teaching, and writing has helped to bring about these exchanges between disciplines. Each book is problem-oriented and evidence-oriented, and none of the authors presume to give final answers to the issues they examine. Although most of the volumes concentrate on elementary and secondary education, many discuss relevant aspects of higher education.

The series as a whole could form the core of introductory or advanced courses in the social, philosophical, or historical foundations of education. But each volume is self-contained, and individual books will be useful in other courses in the education curriculum that analyze the American school system and the basic educational issues of our society. Since many such issues covered in the series have implications far beyond those of education, many of the books will provide supplementary reading for courses outside the department or school of education, especially in the behavioral and social sciences and in social and intellectual history. The books of the series will also serve as useful additions to professional libraries of individuals and school systems.

The present volume, *Understanding Children of Poverty*, has as its authors two sociologists with career-long interests in the sociology of education and in the culture and society of the deprived sector of the American population. They provide a penetrating summary and analysis of the contributions sociologists have made toward understanding the culturally deprived child in the context of the family, the social life of the community, the employment market, the school as a social institution, and the classroom within the school. The authors bring to this analysis their own research and applied contributions, covering the rural as well as the urban problem, and their experience with actual demonstration programs as well as with theoretical studies. Though addressed to teachers and educators, the book does not attempt to deal directly with specific teaching methodologies, or to provide a summary of typical programs for the deprived. The attempt, rather, is to develop an understanding of and general approach to deprived youth. In the words of the authors, the book is organized around the following ideas: "the degree and nature of deprivation in our society; conditions that appear to foster deprivation or enhance 'success'; and possible methods of dealing with these conditions in the school setting." At all times the approach is realistic and tentative. The authors write with full recognition of how little we know about working successfully with the deprived; thus they reject any particular dogma. Recurrent themes throughout the book — iterated most clearly in Chapter Five — are concerned with the goals of deprived youth: what their goals are and how these goals relate to the goals of the school and society. They emphasize most strongly the need for congruence between the goals of the youth and the goals of the teacher, the need for youth to see that the teacher desires to help them attain their goals, and the need for the teacher to be perceived as someone who has the ability to help them attain their goals.

In the opening chapter the authors present the argument that the school is the best-prepared institution in our society for undertaking the task of socializing the children of poverty — regardless of how inadequate our schools may currently seem for handling the enormous difficulties of this task. The authors proceed to a careful definition of the meaning of cultural deprivation within the context of the concepts of values, norms, and sanctions of culture. An extensive treatment is then given to the interrelated elements of deprivation — in education, in employment, and in social status and prestige. Chapter Two deals with the socialization of deprived children in the family and the immediately surrounding society. Case studies are provided which poignantly illustrate the condition of the poor, and a contrast is offered between the values and goals of the poor and those of the middle class, including the contrast in attitudes toward education and the promotion of education. Chapter Three provides a discussion of the relation between school performance and deprivation, including an analysis of the lack of congruence between the goals of deprived youth and the goals and practices of the school. Topics treated include the use of intelligence measures, the analysis of character formation in relation to school performance, and the effects of the home environment upon school performance. In Chapter Four the authors deal more directly with classroom experiences, providing analyses of the attitudes of teachers, discipline, instruction, and the aims and functions of education. In the final chapter the authors develop more fully their position concerning the congruence of goals between teacher and student that is required if the teacher is to be truly successful in socializing deprived youth. A general approach to the education of the culturally deprived is presented, based upon an individual advisory system, with illustrations from experience in the Job Corps.

Both authors are eminently qualified by training and experience to undertake the sociological analysis presented in this volume. Dr. David Gottlieb received his training in sociology at Wayne State University as an undergraduate and at the University of Chicago in doctoral studies. He has held academic appointments at Northwestern University, the University of Chicago, Michigan State University, and Howard University. He left his post of associate professor of sociology at Michigan State University in 1964 to become Director of Research and Evaluation of the Job Corps in the Office of Economic Opportunity and has since been promoted to the position of Assistant Director for Plans and Programs in that same organization, a position he currently holds. He has authored and coauthored many books and articles on the sociology of education, adolescent behavior, and youth cultures. He has specialized in survey research methods and techniques and has directed a number of research studies relevant to the topics of this volume. In addition, he has served as a consultant to a number of governmental offices, private agencies, and institutions of higher education on problems related to disadvantaged youth, adolescent rehabilitation, and school integration.

Professor Charles E. Ramsey received his undergraduate training at Indiana State Teachers College, followed by master's and doctoral study in sociology at the University of Wisconsin. He has held academic posts successively at the University of Wisconsin, the University of Minnesota, Cornell University, and Colorado State University and is currently professor of sociology at the University of Minnesota. He has authored and coauthored a number of books and articles on the sociology of youth, research methodology, social change and stratification, and demography. He is a specialist in rural sociology. In addition, he has interests in the sociology of developing countries and has undertaken studies in Puerto Rico and Costa Rica.

I am personally grateful to the authors of this volume for their lucid and encompassing analysis of the position of the deprived in American education. In the past few years there has been a flood of publications on understanding and educating the culturally disadvantaged — most of them edited volumes of scattered articles and conference report papers, often of uneven quality or limited point of view. This little volume has great value as a summary of sociological research and analysis applied to understanding children of poverty, enlivened by the personal experiences and convictions of two research sociologists who have been working daily with the deprived.

JUDSON T. SHAPLIN

Foreword

Our nation, if it is to survive, must absorb and integrate its youth into the workings of adult society. A nation that assigns a significant segment of its population to the sidelines is courting social and economic chaos. Various institutions and agencies are responsible for educating our youth to the role of productive, adult citizenship. In the past the family was the most important agent in this socialization process. Changes in our economy and the demand for more workers with specialized skills have brought about a shift in the cast of persons and agencies actually participating in the training and education of our youth. Obviously, as the needs of society alter, the functions of its institutions change.

During the past three decades the school has played a role of increasing importance in the total education of young people. The school does more than teach reading, writing, and arithmetic; it affects the values, attitudes, and perceptions of its students, and this influence becomes even more pervasive as young people spend more and more time in school.

Despite constant harassment, our schools have done a fairly adequate job of preparing youth for the adult world. Even after openly rebelling against school and teachers and faithfully conforming to adolescent norms and values, the majority of American schoolchildren become law-abiding, tax-paying members of their community. Although we may criticize suburban America, we can safely predict that its future citizens will not be prone to outbursts of violence, acts of civil disobedience, or conditions of unemployment and family disorganization. The prognosis, however, for a smaller but significant number of American children is not so favorable. For the child who comes from a background of poverty — the product of economic and social deprivation — the future is bleak.

The purposes of this book are threefold: first, to introduce the reader to the world of poor children; second, to provide some insights into the poor child's perceptions of himself, his teacher, his peers, and the formal educational process; and, third, to show that poor children do not choose to be alienated or to live in isolation from the mainstream of American life. We are convinced that the children of the poor have both the desire and the potential to succeed in our society. Hopefully, this book will contribute something of value to those who teach and work with America's children.

DAVID GOTTLIEB
Washington, D.C.

CHARLES E. RAMSEY
St. Paul, Minnesota

Contents

Chapter One: THE NATURE AND EXTENT OF DEPRIVATION

In various decades Americans have shown some concern about economic and social deprivation. The plight of the poor and the rejected has been the subject of rousing messages from the pulpit, press, and lectern. Poverty and low income, low educational attainment, low quality of education, the exploitation of the laboring class, the welfare class, the disadvantaged, minority groups, and the farmer have all at one time or the other been objects of concern. Each of the problems or problem groups has been the target of action programs designed to alter or hopefully eliminate the offending situation.

It is also characteristic that, in dealing with social problems, Americans have placed primary emphasis on improving the status of the young. The concern for youth has ranged from the humanitarian to the less altruistic view that something must be done to minimize the number of dollars that those who "have" must pass down to those who "have not."

Programs to aid disadvantaged youth in some way or another have been found in each of the five basic social institutions of our society: (1) In the family, programs have usually been initiated within the setting of some other institution: for instance, governments have passed legislation concerning child neglect, or PTAs and governmental agencies have sponsored programs of hot lunches at school. (2) In the educational institution, programs have been implemented within the school itself: curricula have been revised to care for the needs of slow learners, or new organizations with an educational function, such as the Job Corps, have been introduced. (3) In the religious institution, programs have been primarily built into supplementary organizations sponsored by the church, such as Boys Town and sports centers in urban slums. (4) In the economic institution, youth have been aided indirectly by governmental and private welfare agencies that have tried to provide training programs and stopgap employment for those unable to find current employment in the private sector. (5) In the governmental institution, the programs have provided not only regulatory aid in enforcing such items as child labor laws, but also social welfare, in enlisting disadvantaged youth into the National Youth Administration in the 1930s and 1940s, and into the Job Corps, the Neighborhood Youth Corps, Operation Head Start, and Upward Bound in the 1960s.

Regardless of the effort of all of the institutions, those most directly responsible for socializing the young—for preparing them to accept adult responsibilities—are the family and the educational institutions. This holds true for the disadvantaged as well as for those enjoying greater opportunity. The resources of the family are meager in the case of most disadvantaged youth —that is, the child who is deprived is deprived primarily because of the limited resources of his family. Thus, help for the disadvantaged child often comes through direct help to his family, through such programs as Aid to Dependent Children (ADA). Usually the assistance is economic—as if economic opportunity were basic to gaining success in American society. The place of the economic factor in maintaining opportunity will be dealt with later, but at this point we can say that the economic factor, though important, is insufficient to explain variations in attaining success in our country.

Presumably and ideally, the resources available to the school for helping the poor child are equal to those available for educating the child who comes from more comfortable surroundings. The accuracy of this statement, as stated, is open to question since schools containing large numbers of children from disadvantaged families will have less funds, older and less attractive buildings, lower teacher salaries, fewer pieces of educational hardware, and frequently teachers with limited professional experience. Schools in primarily Negro districts and schools in rural areas are examples of the discrepancy between the ideal and the reality.

Nevertheless, resources are distributed more equally among schools than among families, if one is to compare these resources on a dollar-per-person basis. State aid to deprived areas has done much to equalize available resources, but the equalization is far from perfect. Even if financial resources were equally distributed, other significant differences would still persist. Teachers of excellence generally prefer teaching in cities to teaching in small isolated rural communities. Furthermore, if sparsely populated areas are to have the same variety of expensive teaching aids and equipment as those found in urban schools, they must get a greater amount of money per pupil. In economic terms, the cost-per-pupil of educational materials is higher for schools with small populations.

Although there is little consensus on how we can most effectively alter the status of poor youth, there is agreement that the task must be largely handled by our schools. Despite differences in resources and quality, schools are better prepared than families to socialize youth and are probably more responsive to change and control. Although "cultural lag" is a recognized problem in American education, the school is so organized that it can implement high-level policy more quickly and uniformly than can the unorganized millions of diverse disadvantaged families. Certainly state-level policy—and to some extent, federal-level policy—can be implemented through established lines of communication, from state departments of education through the superintendent's office down to the school principals and teachers in the classroom. There are no such foremen supervising family activities.

The close resemblance between the school and the real world is yet another reason why the school is better able to train the disadvantaged. In the family, the individual is often loved and forgiven his transgressions as an individual. He is not judged according to impersonal criteria or standards; he is not a statistic. In school as in life, on the other hand, impersonal standards and criteria are usually the basis for judging an individual's actions, and although competition and impersonal evaluation may be tempered by some concern for the individual as an individual, few teachers would go to the extent of falsifying grades to help a "deserving" youth. Rather, the teacher would, at the most, help the individual study in order to compete on the basis of impersonal criteria. Many disadvantaged children, moreover, come from families where few standards are imposed. Too often they get little experience in performing tasks and fulfilling responsibilities, and rarely are they introduced to patterns of stability and regularity. The school, for these children at least, may be the one source which teaches them the importance of meeting obligations and introduces them to a continuous and fairly consistent way of life.

A final reason why the school is central to any strategy for modifying the inequalities among youth is that educational achievement is basic to the future success of an individual. Regardless of how much an individual truly learns, knows, or understands, his measured levels of educational achievement—in the form of degrees and diplomas—are essential ingredients in almost every facet of adult life. It is usually not so much the actual quality of his education or his ability that matters, but rather the formal level attained and the degree held. Although many well-paying jobs and professions require no set number of years of formal education, entry into most prestigious occupations and life styles requires educational credentials, despite their questionable validity. The task, then, is to keep young people in schools for as long a period of time as possible and at the same time, hopefully, provide them with a meaningful, high-quality educational program. Although important to all young people, educational achievement becomes essential for the poor child who can expect little in the way of family support or assistance as compensation for educational deficiencies.

The relations between education and the conditions of disadvantaged youth are thus the appropriate subject for discussion in this book, which is organized around the following ideas: the degree and nature of deprivation in our society; conditions that appear to foster deprivation or enhance "success"; and possible methods of dealing with these conditions in the school setting. We cannot claim that the proposed methods will necessarily work, but given the conditions analyzed in the early parts of this volume, they seem to represent the most promising guidelines for working out a more detailed methodology.

THE MEANING OF CULTURAL DEPRIVATION

An elementary assumption held by those concerned with the disadvantaged is that American ideology puts a prime value on equality. The ideal of equality is far from perfectly practiced (if one were to infer values from behavior, one could even seriously question whether Americans really value equality), but we would contend that, with certain qualifications, equality is a basic American value.

We must first qualify the word *equality* by saying that, as expressed in our fundamental documents and beliefs, it refers not to an assumption of equal performance, an equal ability to perform, or equal rewards for unequal performance, but rather to equality of *opportunity*. The "self-evident" truths of the Declaration of Independence included the idea "that all men are created equal"—but equal only in their rights to life, liberty, and the *pursuit* of happiness, not necessarily its attainment. Therefore one cannot refer to equality without reference to the idea of opportunity.

The second qualifier follows upon the first. Included in the idea of equality is the American criterion of "fair play" or fairness. One should accept defeat or failure so long as the judgments on which the defeat and failure were based were fair; that is, the person or team should have an equal opportunity to win or lose.

The third qualifier is more serious: many people do not agree that equal opportunity—or fairness—applies to all persons or all groups in all situations.

The opportunity for a Negro to play in major league baseball was equalized only after World War II. The equal opportunity for a Negro to buy a house in an area of his own choosing is found only in some sections of a few cities in the United States. These denials of opportunities exist not only in fact but in word—many Americans are vocally opposed to equal opportunity in housing, just as many Americans spoke out against equality in baseball before the 1940s.

If the argument stated above is granted, then the problem of deprivation or disadvantage becomes one of the discrepancies between ideal and practice, between the ideal of equal opportunity that we profess to value and the actual measure of equal opportunity that we show in our behavior. If a person from a slum family earns less money because he refuses to acquire money-making skills, then the problem may be his and not necessarily a serious social problem. But if that person earns less money because the avenue to more money is barred to him for irrelevant and prejudicial reasons, then a serious social problem exists in living up to the value placed on equality of opportunity. That the latter is often the case will be documented in the succeeding chapters.

Cultural deprivation implies another basic feature of American society. Competition, which is both valued and implemented quite effectively as the means toward goals, is intimately linked to equality of opportunity, for it is in competition that equality of opportunity is enforced or withheld. But competition for what? The goals which Americans compete for are a part of the culture of the American people.

The Meaning of Culture

Deprivation or *disadvantage* is a term implying a value judgment. It implies that various individuals or groups are hindered—some more, some less—in competing for certain valued ends of society. The sum total and the meaning of these values constitute much of American culture.

In defining the term, we must say first that *culture includes goals or values that are states or conditions toward which we are obliged to strive.* In America we must strive to gain a livable income, a reasonable education, a fair degree of prestige or respect from others, a comfortable house, a minimum diet, the money and will to go to a physician when we are ill, and the like. Two principles are especially important in understanding how cultural goals or values affect deprived youth: (1) Most people in American society internalize these goals as morally right, even obligatory, and a person so conditioned will feel guilty if he fails to attain a level of achievement deemed satisfactory by his fellows. (2) Since goals or values are internalized as morally right, a person's failure to achieve such ends will draw moral indignation from his fellows. Even though they may compete with him and help bring about his failure, they will lose respect for him to the extent that he generally fails. This loss of respect may contribute psychologically to his tendency to fail in future situations.

Second, *culture includes means or norms as well as goals.* These means or norms are always limited in any culture. In America an obvious example of such a limitation would be the taboo against stealing as a means of achieving the end of a livable income. A more subtle limitation of the not-too-distant past involved equating a "good hard day's work" with physical labor and associating intellectual pursuits with pomposity or polished idleness. Even today blue-collar workers and farmers refer with a certain degree of derogation to the "boys in white shirts." Perhaps the low prestige attached to the used-car salesman, for instance, is based on a concept of honesty that does not fit present-day marketing realities. Nevertheless, regardless of the definition of work—physical, mental, or social—its value as a means of livelihood is still fundamental. Even during the widespread unemployment of the Great Depression of the 1930s, guilt and moral indignation were attached to welfare. To make use of means unfavored by the culture or to fail to make use of means prescribed as right both constituted "wrongs."

Third, in addition to ends or values and means or norms, *culture includes sanctions.* Sanctions consist of rewards for conforming to cultural values and norms and of punishments for failing to conform. In the case of legal norms—those written into statutes, executive orders, and common law—the sanctions are reasonably precise, although the range of punitive discretion exercised by a judge can admittedly be great. In the case of the violation of unwritten norms—such as the failure of poverty groups to attain a reasonable income—the sanctions are not precise. Since they are implicit rather than explicit, they are often far in excess of the seriousness of the violation. For example, one of the first things Americans wish to know in meeting a stranger is his occupation. Probably most teachers would react in much the same way as most other professionals when they learn that the new acquaintance is unemployed or on welfare. Even the person who is "fair" and "unprejudiced" and who recognizes that unemployment is not always the choice of the unemployed will often feel that he does not wish to pursue the friendship further.

The tightly organized system of ends, means, and sanctions is such that success begets success and failure begets failure. The person who exhibits the rewards of achievement—well dressed, well housed, and well paid—enjoys further privileges because he is able to wear his rewards. Not only does the poor person tend to perpetuate his low income and other disadvantages but he tends to pass his disadvantages on to the next generation. Unless there is some intervention or social change, most children from welfare families will be on welfare rolls as adults.

In using the term *cultural deprivation* then, we give culture a meaning involving three elements: (1) Values are those cultural ends considered by most people to be obligations and criteria for judging others. To the extent that a person fails to attain certain valued ends, he attracts criticism and becomes subject to further disadvantage. (2) *Norms* are those cultural elements that limit and prescribe the means by which a person can achieve the culturally prescribed goals. Failure to use the available means or resort to means considered taboo can stimulate guilt and moral indignation. (3) *Sanctions* constitute the system of rewards and punishments used to regulate the achievement or nonachievement of ends or the correct or incorrect use of means. Often sanctions for past failures further discourage a person from achieving future ends or making full use of available means.

The Meaning of Deprivation

Deprivation itself means the state of being dispossessed or divested of some valued condition. Failure to attain the ends prescribed by the culture would represent the substantive nature of cultural deprivation, and the importance of attaining an elementary level of ends—such as the mundane pleasures of a comfortable house and a minimum diet—is sufficient to justify our working with the deprived. Presumably, the value placed on equality of opportunity should, at least theoretically, apply to the opportunity to invest in the stock market, drive a sports car, or play golf in the afternoon. In the present volume, however, we will deal only with the basic or minimum levels of social status. Our concern will be with those in our society who are not the skilled, or even the blue-collar workers who enjoy at least the security and dignity of full-time employment. Rather, our focus will be on those children who are part of the one-fifth of the American people who live in poverty.

Deprivation refers not only to living in poverty but to being barred from prescribed means for achieving valued ends. Disadvantaged youth attend low-quality schools, they have difficulty attending college, and they get less family support in education. These are but three examples of the many ways in which adequate means are withheld from deprived youth.

FELT NEEDS AND DEPRIVATION. The concept of deprivation implies that the individuals in question fail in competition not because they want to or because they value any less what other Americans value, but because they are unable to achieve. Severe limitations within the social system inhibit their chances of achieving even though they wish to achieve. Two qualifiers, however, must be attached to this statement. Although the term *deprived* cannot be applied to persons *unwilling* to make a livable wage, it certainly can be applied to their offspring, who are incapable of making such a decision. Second, the resignation or despair of poor people should not be mistaken for a lack of desire to achieve; it should not be misinterpreted necessarily as a distaste for education, income, and a more comfortable style of living.

The concept of "felt needs" refers to an individual's awareness that he lacks something he would like to possess and that he is willing to take action and mobilize his resources toward attaining the value. In discussions of foreign aid the concept has been involved in the question of whether the people in underdeveloped countries want the aid offered by the United States.

The same question can be asked of deprived youth: Do they want the help that is offered? To be sure, there is incontrovertible evidence that deprived youth—and their parents—do not eagerly rush to take advantage of the opportunities presented them. Although large numbers have participated in such programs as the Job Corps and Operation Head Start, many more have avoided enrolling in them. Many who participate drop out and return home with few employment opportunities or achievement alternatives. Directors of new educational programs designed specifically for low-income youth are often forced to accept middle-class youth or concentrate on the cream of the poor lest the programs go out of existence. Such evidence is often cited by those who assume that "poor people are poor because they are lazy" or "the unemployed don't want to work."

The other side of the argument—and one we favor—is that the culturally deprived are not truly satisfied with their lot. Such a viewpoint is based on at least three assumptions:

1. The system of disadvantages is such that the poor must either spend all their energies trying to pull themselves up or resign themselves to accepting their current status. Therefore, resignation in the face of seemingly overwhelming odds is a better description of their attitude than are the usual clichés cleverly espoused during afternoon cocktails.

2. The alternatives available to them in seeking more material and nonmaterial comfort are not meaningfully perceived by them as available, relevant, or workable. This distorted perception is often difficult to understand fully. Perhaps the best analogy for a student is the difference between what is said by the teacher and what is heard by the student.

3. The simple question—Are the disadvantaged where they wish to be?—is phrased in a manner not fruitful for scientific study. The question should be enlarged: What types of attitudinal and value frames exist among the deprived? How do their perceptions of opportunities vary? What proportion of the deprived have the various types of attitudes and perceptions? And under what conditions do these variations develop?

RELATIVE DEPRIVATION. Complicating any attempt to analyze and make plans for the culturally deprived is the fact that deprivation is a relative term. What may be considered a level of deprivation in one group or society may not be so considered in another. The level of deprivation is higher, for instance, in the United States than in most other nations and higher in some regions of the

United States than in others. A person whose chances of getting into college are slim, for instance, will feel this deprivation much more strongly if he knows that his society esteems a college education and if he is surrounded by people suffering from the same limitations.

In the United States, although the level below which deprivation occurs has been rising in terms of income levels, educational attainment, access to medical care, length of life, and good health, there are still ecological variations. A high school diploma, for example, may be necessary in an urban center as a requirement for employment as a secretary, but not necessary in a rural area where fewer girls with high school diplomas are available to fill such positions. Variations in standards thus make generalizations about the United States, or even one state, most difficult.

Another complicating factor is that seldom in American history has there been such concern for the problems of deprivation during a period when most of the population has been experiencing affluence. The increasing levels of educational attainment, income, and standards of living, as well as employment, have led many people even to question whether concern for the plight of the poor is legitimate. Indeed, many professionals and businessmen were sincere when they questioned whether, in initiating the war on poverty, anyone would be able to find poverty. The doubt stemmed partly from their tendency to see only the affluence in America (poverty is not always visible en route between the bank and the country club). But the doubt was due partly to an unconscious twisting of facts: they simultaneously decried government intervention in the economic enterprise, denied the existence of poverty, and complained of swollen welfare rolls.

To doubt that deprivation exists is not necessarily to be motivated by either self-interest or a conscious or unconscious desire to twist facts for the sake of an overpowering philosophy of conservatism. Perhaps the most prevalent motivation results from an awareness that poverty aid, when offered, does not always find takers. If such is the case, maybe there is no need for aid; the extent of deprivation may be exaggerated. Many people have arrived at such a conclusion—honestly so. In contemplating the establishment of free legal services in Philadelphia in 1966, for instance, the Philadelphia Bar Association made a survey study that indicated that people do not often accept free legal aid—just as opponents of the aid had contended. What the study also proved, however, is that the poor were unaware of how to use legal counsel— even though, significantly, they had greater need for it than most other people. Being somewhat "trouble prone" (as the director of the study termed them), the poor needed an attorney not only to stay out of jail but also to contend with landlords, welfare agencies, and other government personnel. Often the head of a low-income family faces repossession of an appliance or automobile after one missed payment. His wages are attached in many cases, and this results in his being fired.[1] The conclusions that we can draw from such studies are that the poor do exist and need aid and furthermore that they must be educated to their needs and the means of solving them.

THE INTERRELATED ELEMENTS OF DEPRIVATION

Education

Acquiring an education is crucial to achieving other goals in American society. It is valued for itself; it is a factor related to gaining respect from others; and it is critical in determining earning power. Many occupations, especially those more desirable in our value system, categorically require certain levels of educational attainment. Thus it is well to discuss the state of educational attainment in the United States today.

Although, with every passing generation, a greater proportion of Americans tend to remain in school for longer periods of time, there were still in 1960 almost five million adults over the age of twenty-five who had not completed a minimum of five years of formal education.[2] And even this figure is an inaccurate index of real educational achievement, for even many high school graduates are functional illiterates. A study of Job Corps enrollees, for instance, indicated that the number of years of education they had received did not reliably indicate how well they might perform in reading or arithmetic. *Where* they received their education—not how much education they received— tended to be a better index of probable performance. Despite the discrepancies between performance and formal education, however, most educators would agree that persons with less than five years of formal education would tend to be illiterate; and this would mean nearly one in ten adults in the United States.

Mere literacy, of course, is not enough. Most occupations (not to mention virtually all colleges and universities) require minimally a high school diploma as the price of admission. Yet in 1960 almost 60 percent of the adult males in the United States had not earned a high school diploma (and only 7.7 percent had completed four or more years of college). About half the adult population, both male and female, withdrew during their sophomore year of high school.[3]

There are slight regional variations. Nowhere in 1960 had at least half the

---

[1] In Philadelphia, even before the study was made, a majority of the members of the local bar association had supported the move to establish twelve free law offices in impoverished neighborhoods. After the study, most of the members originally opposing the plan reversed their stand; the American Trial Lawyers Association dropped its opposition; and the American Bar Association went on to ask Congress to double the legal-aid budget of the Office of Economic Opportunity, at a beginning figure of $52 million.

[2] U.S. Bureau of the Census, *U.S. Census of Population, 1960;* Vol. I, *Characteristics of the Population;* Part 1, *United States Summary* (Washington: Govt. Printing Office, 1964), p. 207.

[3] *Ibid.*

adults aged twenty-five or older finished high school, but the West did have almost 49 percent of its adults graduating, in contrast to about 36 to 40 percent in Northeastern and North Central states. The South had the lowest measure of educational attainment, with only 15 percent of its males and 29 percent of of its females completing high school.[4] (Except in the West, the education of females always exceeded that of males.) Some differences also exist between urban, suburban, and rural populations: nationwide, urbanites acquire one or two years more schooling than farm dwellers, and suburbanites two or three more years than urban people.[5] Interestingly enough, if the overall educational level of a region is low (as in the South), the gap between urban and rural educational attainment is wider. The reason may be that Negroes often outnumber whites in these rural areas, and nonwhites customarily receive less education than whites. Indeed, in every state, region, and age group, and among both men and women, nonwhites show greater educational deficiencies.

Because in most states students are not legally required to attend school after reaching the age of sixteen, there is a rather natural, sudden rise in the number of dropouts at that age (a rise of about 10 to 15 percent[6]); obviously, many such students have simply waited for the legal age to abandon their formal education. Again, deprivation is involved. Nonwhites lead whites in the number of dropouts at age sixteen (13 percent nonwhites compared with 11 percent whites). Students with parents whose employment is uncertain or whose occupations have a low status tend toward a higher dropout rate. Students most likely to stay in school, for instance, are those whose fathers are employed and whose mothers are not. Less likely to remain in school are those whose mothers work and whose fathers do not, and least likely are those whose parents are both unemployed. Suburban youth top the list of those most likely to remain in school, whereas youth from slums and impoverished rural areas are at the bottom. Obviously the status of the parents influences the school behavior of the child—illustrating the old maxim that "the apple does not fall far from the tree."

Employment

From what has been said, it is apparent that not only does education affect employment but employment affects education. If a person receives little schooling, he can expect only marginal employment; and, being unemployed or poorly employed, he passes on to his children poor chances of getting a quality education and good employment. Employment—or, more specifically,

---

[4]U.S. Bureau of the Census, *U.S. Census of Population, 1960; Subject Reports; Educational Attainment*, Final Report PC(2)-5B (Washington: Govt. Printing Office, 1963), p. 43.

[5]*Ibid.*, p. 17.

[6]*Ibid.*, p. 752.

income—affects in general the kinds of lives that people can expect to lead. It provides the measure of social prestige as well as the means for acquiring possessions that so many Americans take for granted. (That a large number of the poor, particularly minority groups, cannot take these things for granted is indicated by statistics from the 1960 census: 26 percent of the families in single-unit dwellings in the United States had no basic plumbing facilities; 25 percent no washing machine; 21 percent no telephone; and 22 percent no automobile.[7])

In the United States, current unemployment rates oscillate between 3 and 5 percent.[8] But unemployment alone is not an adequate index of deprivation in income. Many families that have one or more members employed earn wages that fall far below the $3000 usually cited as the amount required for a minimum standard of living.[9] Indeed, in 1960 almost one-third of American families were reported to have total annual incomes of less than $3000.[10] Their future, too, is far from bright. Although many people assume that more government spending or more economic investments in general should raise incomes and increase employment, economists will argue that such expenditures will not affect most low-income families. Even if the national defense budget were doubled, says the director of the Office of Economic Opportunity, the income of 30 million people would remain unaffected. The reason given is that the money would go into activities requiring highly skilled personnel, and low-income families—whose low income is largely due to lack of skills—would remain out in the cold. In fact, their *relative* deprivation could intensify as their incomes remained static and the incomes of other people rose.

Social Status and Prestige

Deprivation is not specifically educational, although educational attainment is a central factor. Neither is it purely a matter of employment. All the status factors are related—when a person is low in one, he is often low in another. The correlation of status characteristics and the presence of distinct

---

[7]U.S. Bureau of the Census, *U.S. Census of Population, 1960; Subject Reports; Persons by Family Characteristics*, Final Report PC(2)-4B (Washington: Govt. Printing Office, 1963), pp. 139–53.

[8]In such statistics, an "unemployed" person is defined by the Bureau of the Census as a person at least fourteen years of age who is out of work and actively seeking employment.

[9]Although the amount required may actually depend on family size, the average minimum usually cited is $3000, which the director of the U.S. Office of Economic Opportunity has reported would provide each person in an average poor family with about 23 cents per meal per day and $1.40 for all other expenses. The figure of $3000, incidentally, is considerably below that used by home management specialists in many states, but it will nevertheless be used in this book when referring to subminimum incomes.

[10]*Characteristics of the Population*, Part 1, p. 225.

classes in many societies has led to the question of class structure in the United States. Are there social classes in a country philosophically dedicated to equality?

The answer to this question is neither clearly yes nor clearly no. Much depends upon the intended meaning of the word *class*. The old Marxian definition—which dichotomized society largely into capitalists and laborers, with only a few peripheral classes related to these two—obviously oversimplifies enormously the status differences in the United States. On the other hand, in spite of our great economic and geographic mobility and in spite of our philosophical dedication to equality, we cannot say that class distinctions are minimal. Perhaps our best approach would be to incorporate sociologist Max Weber's definition of *social honor* into our meaning of *class*. Though recognizing economic classes, Weber also recognized that people classified one another according to the social honors of family, leadership, profession, and other social variables. A key index of social honor would be, Who has dinner with whom, and where?

Sociologists have often resorted to tests calling upon members of a group or community to rate one another according to their individual ideas of social-class standing. Interestingly enough, the ideas are fairly consistent; more often than not, people seem to agree on how any one person should be classed, and they agree fairly well on the reasons for the classification. What differences exist are usually subjective. A banker and a janitor may see the class position of a few people somewhat differently. A rater, for personal reasons, may not use the same criteria to measure two people or two families. One family may be rated on its prestigious history, another on its money, and another on its morality. In a research study of a small rural community, the testers found that about ten different criteria were variously employed in measuring high social standing and about nine were used for relegating persons to a low social standing:[11]

CRITERIA OF HIGHER STANDING

A. *Money, wealth, high material level of living.* This category was the most easily recognized and unambiguous. The answers tended to run to the stereotyped form, more money, but a number of alternative phrasings and nuances appeared.

Better fixed

Better place to live in

Don't have to work or do anything

Wealthy

Financially higher standing

Well-to-do

Own their own homes

Inherited a lot

Have things up to date

[11]Adapted from Otis Dudley Duncan and Jay W. Artis, *Social Stratification in a Pennsylvania Rural Community*, Pennsylvania Agriculture Experimental Station Bulletin No. 543 (University Park: Pennsylvania State College, 1951), pp. 16–19.

B. *Activity and leadership.* The central emphasis here was on civic interest and activity, with a subemphasis in a small minority of the responses on power and influence.

Takes part in more things
Civic activity, such as leaders
Very active in community affairs

Has more to do and say about
  the clubs and organizations
Social activities
Seems to be into everything

C. *Religious worthiness.* These responses stressed participation in church activities and living a Christian way of life.

Good church worker
A good Christian life

Good religious life
Does a lot of church work

D. *Positive moral characteristics.* The leading ideas here were friendliness and neighborliness, sobriety and industriousness, and general high moral character.

Always helping others
Good neighborliness
Tries to get along — honest
Honesty and loyalty
Have amounted to more and
  help others

A better life so that you
  are an example to others
Friendly with everyone
Industrious, sober, neighborly
High morals, good lives

E. *Education.* The attainment of a high educational level and the exercise of training in one's occupation.

A good education and can hold a good position
Better education — kids all graduated from high school
More highly educated

F. *Old families.* Belonging to a family of good name and resident in the community for a long time.

Older residents
Family name

Longer time in community

G. *Usurpation.* The explicitly expressed notion that higher standing is partially or largely a matter of pretensions to such a position.

They think they are better
A lot is just thinking you are

Because they think so
Some put on a front

H. *Occupation.* Mention of occupational status as a condition of higher standing, primarily in reference to doctor, minister, teacher, and businessman.

Is a doctor
Higher because of profession
Better job
Businessman has higher standing

Professional — preacher
In business
Minister and schoolteacher
  have higher standing

I. *Personality.* Desirable personality traits, or the pleasant, likable sort.

Pleasant disposition
Talks better than I can —
  lots of friends

Personality
Sociable, agreeable, not
  snooty

J. *Miscellaneous.* The following is a virtually complete listing of the responses coded as miscellaneous; many of these responses, if more fully qualified, doubtless could have been coded in the preceding categories. The ideas of social prominence and standing of associates could well have been made the basis of another category, except for the small number of responses involved.

Not handicapped — smaller families

Better prepared for the work they're doing

If you have good health, you're pretty well off

Better view of life

Higher socially

Up-to-date farmers who are younger

People they associate with

Social standing in community; way people look up to them; environment, experience — more talent

More prominence — great sportsman

Way of living

Better position socially

High social standing

CRITERIA OF LOWER STANDING

A. *Poverty, poor material level of living.*

Poor people

Have a hard time getting along

Don't have enough to eat, poor housing

Not well off

Isn't doing very well

On relief

No money

B. *Immorality.* The principal traits mentioned referred to drinking, criminality, illicit sexual relations, and general immorality.

Unmarried mothers

Disreputable character

Steal, not trustworthy

Run around with other men

Drink and gamble

Drunkard

Husband in prison

Liars and troublemakers

C. *Irresponsibility.* The main items concerned family neglect, lack of ambition and effort, and carelessness with money.

Don't provide for their families

No attempt to get ahead — just exist

Sponging on government

Choose to be lower — spend money foolishly

Don't feed the kids; out till morning; don't pay bills

They just won't work

Too damn lazy to do anything

Lack of self-respect

D. *Not active in community life.*

No civic interest

Poor attitude toward community betterment

Don't take active part in welfare organization

Doesn't associate with other people

E. *Irreligious.*

Never go to church

Won't even let their children go to Sunday school

People with no religion at all

Unchristian

F. *Lack of education.*

No education

Never see them in school

Can't read or write

Aren't as well educated

G. *Dirty.*
Filthy, dirty   Just plain sloppy
Live like hogs   Not neat and clean

H. *Dull mentality.*
Mentally deficient, with many   Lacking in ability
    children in same shape   Feebleminded
Aren't very intelligent

I. *Misfortune, lack of opportunity.*
Bad luck   Lots of sickness
Never got a good start in   Didn't get the breaks
    life

People in a community rate one another on the basis of such criteria, and they treat one another accordingly, granting or withholding privileges as the case may be. Respondents are indeed willing to place people in "classes"—such as upper, upper-middle, lower-middle, upper-lower, and lower-lower. In this sense, therefore, we may conveniently refer to social classes and to higher and lower ratings that are socially meaningful and that can predict the behavior of a person and the behavior of others toward him.

In one important sense, admittedly, the word *class* is not appropriate in categorizing the population of the United States. Unlike traditional class or caste systems, American classes are not easily discernible, disjunct, and separate groups, and the actions of persons in one class are not distinct from those of persons in other classes. Status variables such as income, educational attainment, and level of living show no sharp breaks. That is to say, there is not a great mass of low-income classes and then a great leap to another large bulk of middle-income classes—with just a few negligible classes in between. Rather, the distribution of income is a gradual curve. Where one class ends and another begins is not easily discernible. The attitudes and behaviors of people overlap regardless of their income or education.

Perhaps the strongest arguments for using the notion of class are that (1) class, as employed in research, is correlated with various behaviors, both of the member of the class and of others toward him, and (2) the status variables are highly correlated.

In the present volume we will not employ the idea of a lower class except as a convenience—particularly in instances when the concept of class has been used in studies of deprivation. Obviously there is need for research that would indicate the extent to which class is an accurate description of the stratification system in the United States. For the time being, however, it is sufficient to note that the idea is useful in some research and analysis, but subject to valid criticism.

No one variable—income, education, or any other element of "social honor"—is so important or so overpowering that it makes *all* the difference in assigning people to one class or another. A person of high income, for instance, may be placed in a disadvantaged position because of immoral behavior or, conversely, be treated with deference even though he ranks low on a few other variables. In other words, all the variables count.

Among the disadvantaged who are the subject of this book, all the status variables not only count but interact. Low income, we have noted, is correlated with occupation and educational attainment. In terms of family prestige the status of the head of the household can play a dramatic role in the success of the child. Most certainly, the range of deprivation is not limited to the world of work and school: the poor have less access to medical and dental care; they are less likely to have the benefit of legal counsel (even though their legal needs exceed those of the middle class); and they are less apt to participate in creative leisure-time activities. The idea of a summer camp, a weekend trip, and visits to Disneyland or the World's Fair is not part of the real world of the poor.

Each of these factors contributes to how the poor child will see himself, his neighborhood, his school, and his community.

In the pages that follow we will take a closer look at the socialization of the disadvantaged child. Our goal will be to provide the reader with certain insights into his family life and background. We hope this information will at least provide the teacher with a better understanding of why some poor youth maintain an attitude of alienation and hostility in their dealings with the educational establishment.

Suggested Readings

BAGDIKIAN, H. BEN. *In the Midst of Plenty.* Boston: Beacon Press, 1964.

GALBRAITH, JOHN KENNETH. *The Affluent Society.* Boston: Houghton Mifflin, 1958.

HARRINGTON, MICHAEL. *The Other America.* New York: Macmillan, 1962.

MILLER, HERMAN P. *Poverty American Style.* Belmont, Calif.: Wadsworth, 1966.

MOORE, TRUMAN. *The Slaves We Rent.* New York: Random House, 1965.

RIESSMAN, FRANK, and others (eds.). *Mental Health of the Poor.* New York: Free Press (a subsidiary of Crowell Collier & Macmillan, Inc.), 1964.

Chapter Two: THE FAMILY AND SOCIAL LIFE OF THE DEPRIVED CHILD

In dealing with the deprived, we are not dealing with any one particular category of low status, such as simple poverty in a strict financial sense. (A rich man can plummet to temporary poverty, but he usually has the knowledge and wherewithal to rise again.) Rather, we are dealing with a combination of low-status variables which, by interacting, prevent individuals from reaching culturally prescribed goals and from fully understanding and using culturally prescribed means. The correlated status variables are those suggested in the preceding chapter: educational attainment, employment and income, and social prestige. To these can be added power, authority, and level of living. It is the interaction and combination of these status variables, when low, that make work with deprived families so difficult and that minimize the degree to which they can alter their own condition.

Statistics suggest these interacting variables. In the mid-1960s, about one in every five families in the United States lived in poverty—if we measure poverty, as we did in the preceding chapter, as a level of income less than $3000 a year for a family of four. Of these poor, 20 percent are estimated to be non-white; indeed, about half the nonwhites in the United States are impoverished by this definition. Geographically, about 50 percent of the poor live in cities, about 16 percent live on farms, and about 30 percent live in rural nonfarm residences. Just less than half live in the South, where a person's chances of being poor are almost twice those of a person elsewhere. Looking at the members of poor families, we find that about 60 percent of the heads of these families completed less than a grade school education, that about one-fourth of these heads are women (who are usually nonwhite), and that about one-third of the heads are over sixty-five and thus generally unemployable. One out of every six youth in America comes from such families. All these statistics suggest the interaction of low income, poor education, racial discrimination, and the disadvantages of socially disapproved family leadership. They also suggest the magnitude of deprivation in the United States.

The frustrations caused by this quantity of deprivation are expressed by the poor in myriad ways, some not so obvious as the infrequent violence or alcoholism or purported "laziness." For instance, despite their meager incomes, many deprived individuals and families purchase television sets, shiny automobiles, or other items that they can seemingly ill afford, considering the straitened circumstances of their food and lodging. Moralists, particularly those who regret the taxes they must pay for aid to the deprived, condemn such "extravagances." But the poor buy these things not out of a miscalculation of their finances, but out of a sense of frustration and a need to try, however superficially, to escape from their situation and to enter the kind of materially comfortable life that our social system values so strongly. Our American system of values, indeed, puts great pressure on the deprived to scrape enough money together for such purchases.

Frustration is also indicated in the deprived youth's extreme tendency to lack intellectual curiosity and interest. All youth, it should be noted, do begin life with natural vitality and interest, eager to explore their environment. Middle-class youth may lose this curiosity if they are subjected at home and in school to norms of "respectability," rote learning, and career orientations; they may rebel and search for means of enjoyment more socially acceptable to adolescents than to adults, whose values may seem rather alien. However, deprived youth, though perhaps not subjected so much to moral dictums and demands for successful careers, tend to lose curiosity and interest because they lack opportunities to apply the curiosity and interest. They live in a narrow environment with few socially acceptable outlets for achievement and enjoyment in life. Curiosity is not washed out of them, as it is out of many middle-class youth; it simply and gradually withers as it gets little chance for expression and development.

WORK PATTERNS OF THE DEPRIVED

Deprived families—particularly those who head them—are frequently alleged to be lazy, and this allegation is extended to their children in school. Because deprived youth tend to study less and achieve less, teachers, principals, and communities too often view them as lazy pupils. The term *lazy* is intended to be not descriptive but explanatory; it accuses them somehow of an inherent fault. Such an accusation, of course, warrants a considerable amount of examination, for, if it were valid, our social system, which tries to motivate people by offering them differential rewards for work achieved, would be out of kilter. What could be done about people who were lazy and unmotivated by rewards and could not care for themselves? To get other people to feel responsible for them would be very difficult.

Perhaps the most understanding and empathetic analysis of the deprived and their alleged laziness was offered many years ago by sociologist Allison Davis. His essay is so instructive that we quote it *in toto*:[1]

> Just as the members of the higher skilled working class and of management act in response to their culture, to their system of social and economic rewards, so do the underprivileged workers act in accord with their culture. The habits of "shiftlessness," "irresponsibility," lack of "ambition," absenteeism, and of quitting the job, which management usually regards as a result of the "innate" perversity of underprivileged white and Negro workers, are in fact *normal responses* that the worker has learned from his physical and social environment. These habits constitute a system of behavior and attitudes which are realistic and rational in *that environment* in which the individual of the slums has lived and in which he has been trained.
>
> My purpose is to trace the origin of these work habits in the social and economic system of the communities in which the underprivileged worker has to live. I shall be specific and concrete.
>
> The evidence will be taken from several studies of white and Negro working-class groups in the Chicago area, studies recently carried out by my colleagues and myself in the University of Chicago. They include evidence on 600 families, both white and Negro. Of these, 200 were middle class, and 400 were working class. In addition, the studies include personal observations and interviewing of selected white and Negro working-class families in their homes, where they were observed several times a week for nearly a year. The intensive studies of Pearl, of Ruth, and of Clark will be used to illustrate the findings of the statistical data dealing with 600 families.
>
> *PEARL AND HER KIN*
> Pearl Elno, the white female worker. At eighteen, Pearl married Jim Elno. Both youngsters were ambitious and smart. They were both good workers, anxious to buy a home of their own, and to get ahead in the world. Jim studied hard at his trade; and he bought a derby hat and a pair of spats — just to show

[1] Reprinted by permission from *ETC: A Review of General Semantics*, Vol. III, No. 4; copyright, 1946, by the International Society for General Semantics.

his friends that he was a man who took himself seriously and intended to get somewhere in the world.

His young wife was always more practical and conscientious than Jim, and forced him to leave his mother's, set up a home of his own, and to work for goals more enduring than a derby and spats. All her efforts for a house of their own and for a decent standard of living were defeated, however, during the next ten years, by the rapidly increasing number of their children. Jim was a Catholic, and Pearl was a very fertile woman. In nine years, she bore seven children.

Unable to secure work during most of the thirties, and presented annually with a new baby by Pearl, Jim began to drink heavily. Any father who has had to come home to five, or six, or seven small children, and has had to try to live and sleep with them, crowded into a three-room flat, will sympathize with Jim, I imagine. During the depression, four children were born to the Elnos. They had to flee to steadily smaller and poorer apartments, and the children were reduced to half-starvation rations, which kept them sorely undernourished and chronically ill. Unemployment and their hopelessly large family wore away the determination and the morale of the parents, especially of Jim. They separated twice, and Jim deserted once but returned. He was arrested two or three times for panhandling while drunk. He beat his wife several times, when he was drunk. The Elnos and their seven little children were on the rocks and seemed headed for the bottom.

But Pearl still had her own parental family. Her father and mother and her sisters, together with their husbands, formed a closely organized and loyal clan, which repeatedly rescued her and her seven children. The sisters took them in when Jim was violently drunk or when they were evicted for inability to pay the rent. They brought the children clothes and helped feed them.

The history of the Elno family illustrates in part how the organization and the typical experiences of the white working-class family control the motivation of the lower-class worker. The actual daily pressure of five to ten hungry stomachs to fill, backs to clothe, and feet to cover forces the working-class parent to reduce his ambitions to this level of subsistence, to lower his sights as far as long-term planning and study for finer skills are concerned, [and] to narrow, limit, and shorten his goals with regard to the care, nutrition, education, and careers of his children.

This terrible pressure for physical survival means that the *child* in the average working-class family usually does not learn the "ambition," the drive for high skills and for educational achievement that the middle-class child learns in his family. The working-class individual usually does not learn to respond to these strong incentives and to seek these difficult goals, because they have been submerged in his family life by the daily battle for food, shelter, and for the preservation of the family. In this sense, ambition and the drive to attain the higher skills are a kind of luxury. They require a minimum *physical security*; only when one knows where his next week's or next month's food and shelter will come from, can he and his children afford to go in for the long-term education and training, the endless search for opportunities, and the tedious apple polishing that the attainment of higher skills and occupational status requires.

Secondly, the Elno family's history illustrates the deprivations, the shocks of fortune, the drain of illness and malnutrition, as well as the social and psychological disorganization, that reduce the efficiency of the underprivileged worker. A society that pens families into this kind of physical and social environment actually cripples both the ability and the work motivation of its workers. If there is one thing that modern psychology makes clear, it is this: men cannot be motivated successfully to work hard, or to learn well, simply by putting the screws upon them.

The masses of working-class people, like the Elnos, cannot be frightened and forced into better work habits, simply through having the economic squeeze put on them, or through being threatened constantly with firing. Such threats do not intimidate them, as they do the middle-class clerk or schoolteacher, because the underprivileged worker is thoroughly accustomed to those conditions of life that middle-class people call "insecurity." Most important of all, he knows he can always "bunk-in" with a relative, usually on his mother's side of the family, and he is certain that an extra plate will be filled for him and his, so long as his relatives have food. The harder the economic noose is drawn, the tighter the *protective* circle of the average working-class family is drawn. Thus economic intimidation is much less effective than with white-collar employees. Since most working-class people do not get the rewards of social and economic prestige in our society, they do not fear the loss of the job or the attendant loss of respectability in their communities nearly so deeply as do the white-collar workers.

RUTH IN A KITCHENETTE

One other example of this pattern of *group* economic help and solidarity should be included, before leaving the matter. In Negro families in the rural South, and generally in those which have migrated from the farms to Chicago, the circle of relations who help each other economically is even larger than in the average white working-class family. There are more children in these families. The bonds of kinship, the closeness of feeling, and the number of mutual duties are also greater in the Negro working-class family owing to its recent experiences as an integrated economic and social unit on the plantations.

There are also many broken white and Negro working-class families, of course. But these individuals, whose families have been scattered by death, disease, desertion, and immigration, are also provided with a communal group, which helps them in times of economic difficulty and illness. The life of Ruth, a Negro worker in Chicago, who was born in Mississippi, illustrates this point.

Ruth's parents were unskilled workers, far below the Elnos in both education and opportunity for occupational training — at the very bottom of the economic hierarchy.

Ruth, her four sisters and brother, and her parents lived in the large cellar of an old tenement on the South Side. The kitchen [was] only an open corner at the back of the cellar, with a small gas stove and a faucet. The nine families shared this corner as their "kitchen." But they had an organized, cooperative system of sharing, which went far beyond the joint use of the so-called "kitchen." They shared the small stocks of furniture, their bedclothes, and their wearing apparel. Most important of all, they shared their food and even their money. When a family was both out of work and off relief, the other families put their money and food into a communal "pot," in which the destitute family shared. This is a hard system to beat, for those who believe in the effectiveness of economic intimidation in making good workers. When workers can survive at this level, and still have the social support and approval of their friends, they can scarcely be threatened or starved into better work habits. They will have to be led by the offering of concrete rewards of better job opportunities and wages and better treatment and status on the job.

When Ruth was fifteen, her parents separated, and her mother remarried. This marriage forced Ruth out of her home at once. The next year she had to leave school and go to work. After she had to leave her home, but before she could obtain her working papers, Ruth lived, slept, and ate with the families of her working-class school friends. Often she had little sleep because there was no bed available, but she had a roof over her and at least a meal a day. She also shared the clothes of her school friends.

This communal group living has persisted, even though Ruth has now been working for more than two years. She is a hard and powerful worker who carries a man's load. Foremen pick her for heavy, driving jobs that not one woman out of ten can stand. She likes to do this heavy work thoroughly, but she also finds it exhausting. Moreover, she is still very young, and she has no responsibilities except herself. Therefore, she stays off the job rather frequently and sometimes misses several days in succession. She can continue this habit, because she still has her group of friends, her large social clique, who are really her "adopted" family and who will give her shelter and food, and lend her clothes whenever they have them. Therefore, Ruth disappears from the job even when she has no money. Keeping her broke, by paying her only every two weeks or every three weeks, will not keep her on the job. She can always "bunk-in" with her group of friends. This is a typical experience of underprivileged workers, both male and female, and both in the South and in the North. Groups of people, who have no families, live together, share food, money, clothes, and beds, and also share their work; for example, trading their ironing for another person's washing or cleaning.

It scarcely needs to be emphasized that this is a way of life that is demoralizing to the individual's habits of work. It is not realized generally, however, that the problems of increasing the efficiency of the underprivileged worker always involves two major kinds of difficulties that must be attacked. First his cultural goals must somehow be raised; his ceiling of aspiration for education, for respectability, for skills, and for better training of his children must become high enough to motivate him to work harder. Such efforts to change their cultural habits and their social status are the driving force behind those relatively few workers who do rise above the slum environments that I have been describing. Because this problem of motivating the lower-class worker to strive hard for more respectable and complex ways of life is the most difficult problem, it will be considered last here.

The other, more immediate, more tangible task for our society in improving the efficiency of the labor supply is that of improving the underprivileged workers' standard of living. Workers who live under the conditions that I have described suffer heavy penalties in loss of sleep, malnutrition, and disease, which in turn greatly reduce their efficiency.

Worst of all, from the point of view of those who wish to change these poor work habits, the slum dwellers become accustomed and "adjusted" to their crippling standards of living. Like people in every class, every culture, they learn to regard their environment and their living habits as decent and satisfying. This is the circle that our society must break, in order to *increase the consciousness of economic needs among the masses of workers*, and thus lead to fuller production and better labor.

Ruth sleeps in a kitchenette apartment rented by a mother with eight children. Ruth shares a bed with five other adolescents and children, sleeping crosswise in the bed. She counts it a windfall when there are only three in the bed, and she may sleep lengthwise. A record of her hours of sleep was kept last winter, for two periods of two weeks each, one in November and one in January. She was in bed an average of 4½ hours out of each 24. During these ten working days, she was absent four. Her work was extremely heavy, so heavy that she was given a half hour's rest by the plant for each hour on the job. Without more sleep, she said, she could not stand the work even five days a week. She has been trying since Christmas to find a room to rent. Last fall she tried to find a kitchenette apartment, so that she could marry, but, as anyone who knows the South Side's residential "lock-in" understands, she had no chance.

Similar conditions prevail among white workers in many parts of the city, of course. In one large area restricted to whites on the South Side, the great majority of *families with children* live in single rooms, or in kitchenette apartments. No matter whether the people in these modern urban ratholes in which human children and their parents must live are white or Negro, the social and economic results are the same. The children are forced out into the streets, day and night; they are "movie children" or completely vagrant children. Life cannot be lived as a family group in these packed rooms; it has to be lived on the streets, in the motion picture theaters, the taverns, the bars, and the night clubs. Under such unimaginable living conditions, all the effort, training, and money, which in the case of the middle-class worker goes into his home, is blocked and diverted to sex, recreation, and gambling. How can a worker be motivated to work to furnish or to improve his home, when he cannot get an apartment, or even a bed to sleep in?

Education, as the underprivileged worker experiences it, likewise differs from the education of middle-class persons. It differs in its length, in its content, and in its value as a social and economic tool. In the Chicago area, the average number of grades completed by white *working-class* mothers is 8.6.

Whereas for the skilled worker and the office person both their drive to work steadily and their interest in developing their skills are powerfully stimulated by their training in school, for the average underprivileged worker, on the other hand, our schools are unrealistic in their methods and in their attempts at motivation. Furthermore, the schools are staffed by highly protected middle-class persons, whose goals and whose economic opportunities are quite different from those of the families and children of the lower class. To the underprivileged worker, an adolescent, the words and the goals of his teacher, those words and goals to which middle-class adolescents react with respect and hard striving, mean very little. For the words of the teacher are not connected to the *acts of training in his home*, with the actual rewards in school, or with actual steps in moving toward a career, which alone can make the words affective in motivating him to learn good school habits. Thus our educational system, which next to the family is the most effective agency in teaching good work habits to middle-class people, is largely ineffective and unrealistic with underprivileged groups. Education fails to motivate such workers because our schools and our society both lack *real rewards* to offer underprivileged groups. Neither lower-class children nor adults will work hard in school or on the job just to please the teacher or boss. They are not going to learn to be ambitious, to be conscientious, and to study hard, as if school and work were a fine character-building game, which one plays just for the sake of playing. They can see, indeed, that those who work hard at school usually have families that already have the occupations, homes, and social acceptance that the school holds up as the rewards of education. The underprivileged workers can see also that the chances of their getting enough education to make their attainment of these rewards in the future at all probable is very slight. Since they can win the rewards of prestige and social acceptance in their own slum groups without much education, they do not take very seriously the motivation taught by the schools.

CLARK GIVES UP TRYING

The impact upon the underprivileged worker of the physical and cultural environment that I have been describing is represented by the case of Clark, a twenty-four-year-old white man, who was intensively interviewed in the Department of Education. Clark was living in basement rooms, bunking in with friends. As conditions became too crowded even for that level of society, or as Clark wore out his welcome, he moved from one such refuge to another. He ate what he would buy with the change he made on odd jobs and what his friends could give him. Except for a meal with friends two or three times a week, he lived on two or three nickel frankfurters or hamburgers a day. For clothes he had one frayed suit made of shoddy and a ragged half-cotton overcoat. He also had two pairs of trousers and two or three shirts, which he left for a time with various friends and which were all eventually stolen.

Clark went to work as a machine operator in a plant. He continued to bunk in with friends for several months. With the wages he earned the first three or four months, he bought chiefly food and clothes, paid his debts to his friends, and got drunk on weekends. As time went on he spent about 75 percent of his income on clothes, liquor, night clubs, and house parties. Less than a week after payday, he usually had to borrow his carfare to get to work and to depend upon his friends for his meals, as well as for a place to sleep.

This behavior was part of a practical cultural system, however. His friends also depended upon him for loans and food, when he had just been paid. Thus, they actually had developed a system of getting money every Friday or Saturday, instead of only every second week on payday. Each worker's payday was in reality a payday that he shared with one to two friends. Thus, each man had a payday every week. Their ideal was a payday every day, so that they would have ready cash always.

Like most of his group, Clark had a regular weekend bout of drunkenness and a series of parties. These lasted through Sunday night, so that he almost never went to work on Mondays. On other nights, he always stayed up until twelve or one o'clock. Since he had to be up by six in order to reach work on time, he averaged less than five hours per night, including weekends. He missed an average of one and one-half days on the job, out of every week — sometimes because he did not have carfare or food, sometimes because his rest was too broken.

After about fifteen months of work, Clark fell in love with a girl, and he began to take more interest in his job. He wanted to become foreman, and began getting up at five o'clock in the morning, so as not to be late for work. He decided to marry the girl and for the first time began to "save" his wages, paying on furniture. He and the girl set out to find a place to live. Finally they discovered a tenement on the railroad tracks where the landlady agreed to rent them two rooms. They returned with their suitcases to find that the landlady had decided she would rent only to men. In two months they were unable to find any other place to live.

Clark is still living with his friends, four to a room, and has given up his plan to marry. He still spends almost all his wages on clothes, liquor, and recreation. He still misses at least three days on the job out of every two weeks. During the four years he has been working, however, there have been three periods when he improved his work habits, his punctuality, and his motivation. The first was when he wanted to marry, and actually was buying furniture, and looking for a home. The second period of improvement occurred later, when Clark was trying to become a foreman, in order to convince his girl's mother that he was not an "ignorant bum," as she claimed. The third period followed his first visit to a meeting of his union, and his resultant interest in winning status within the union. Each of these situations was a powerful stimulus to Clark's motivation on the job. From them we can learn what makes him work more effectively.

First, however, what made him *fail* to work well? During these three periods when he actually wished to become an efficient worker and tried to change his habits, why did he gradually lose his drive and return to his old habits? The reasons seem clear enough. First, like Ruth, the colored worker, he was influenced powerfully by the fact that he had no home and was unable to find one. The effort of both these workers to find a home, so that they could marry, was blocked by our chaotic housing situation. A society in which a large proportion of the population cannot find a home — cannot even rent a home from the people who own them — is in this basic respect less well organized than most "primitive" societies. If people cannot find a place for themselves and for their families to live as a group, and to live fairly decently, according to their lives, their motivation to work hard is severely weakened. If the young adults cannot find a home, they usually cannot marry. Since marriage is one of the most powerful drives in motivating workers to accept responsibility and to "settle down," our housing situation is demoralizing to work habits.

Secondly, Clark failed in his desire to become a foreman, because both the habits he had learned and especially his lack of education made him unfit for this responsibility. He had gone only to the sixth grade, and he had not learned well what was taught in those grades. Like millions of underprivileged workers, he could barely write a sentence, even an ungrammatical sentence. Simple addition and subtraction were laborious problems for him. This educational handicap, plus the great mental and nervous strain created by the improvement of his habits (of course, his hours of going to bed and getting up, of his application to his work, of making time every day), is too great for nine out of ten individuals in his position to overcome.

Third, the same educational deficiencies and cultural habits which prevented his improving his status in the plant likewise make it impossible for him to attain any status in his union. The local, he found, was run by workers who were a step above him in social status, who were at the *top* level of lower-class groups and sometimes were in the lower-middle class. They had skills and habits with which he could not compete. He soon gave up this hope also, and thus this third powerful incentive to change his work habits was extinguished.

The most powerful of all the forces that keep him in his present way of life and of work are the pleasures that he actually can attain by following his underprivileged culture. He gets strong biological enjoyment. He spends a great deal of his nights in sexual exploration, since he does not have to go to work the next day. He lives in a social world where visceral, genital, and emotional gratification is far more available than it is in a middle-class world. Recreation, relaxation, and pure laziness from Friday night through Sunday night are extremely satisfying experiences. If such a weekend leaves the worker too exhausted to get on the job Monday or even Tuesday and causes him to lose $10 or $15, it nevertheless is so organically rewarding that he will repeat the experience the following weekend, or certainly the following payday.

Such are the emotional, the cultural, and the economic determinants of the work habits of the underprivileged worker. He lives in a different economic and social environment from that in which the skilled and the middle-class workers live. Therefore, the behavior that he learns, the habits that are stimulated and maintained by his cultural group, are different also. The individuals of these different socio-economic statuses and cultures are reacting to different realistic situations and psychological drives. Therefore, their values and their social goals are different. Therefore, the behavior of the underprivileged worker, which the boss regards as "unsocialized" or "ignorant" or "lazy" or "unmotivated," is really behavior learned from the socio-economic and cultural environments of these workers. In a realistic view, we must recognize it to be perfectly normal, a sensible response to the conditions of their lives.

If we wish to change these habits — and they are a great burden upon our production — we must offer the underprivileged worker real rewards. They must be sufficiently powerful to repay him for the hard work and self-denial required to change his old habits, and to compete with the rewards of a physical kind that he already gets.

What are these real goals, for which he will work harder? The first is a place to live, a place that is not merely a kitchenette apartment, or a basement room, or a corner in a cellar, with three to six people to a bed. It has to be a place that appears desirable in the eyes of the underprivileged worker, a place he will "go for." This in turn means acceptance of responsibility and the getting up of long-term goals. And these require good, steady work.

Neither a home for the rearing of a family nor the development of good work habits can be attained in a year or two. The underprivileged worker's goals are short-term because his hold upon a job and upon clothes and upon food is short-term. He knows well that he cannot establish a home, buy furniture, begin buying a house, all the endeavors that keep middle-class people busy and conscientious, in a year or two. He cannot educate his children, even through high school, on a few years of good wages. That is what is meant by the words "economic and social security" to the middle-class person, namely, that there is an excellent chance that his work career and income will be steady and adequate to meet his standard of living. This is the kind of security possessed by middle-class people.

For the worker, short periods of good wages and plentiful jobs do not take the place of this security. One cannot change his way of living, or [prompt him to] buy a home or educate his children, on this kind of income. To have a chance to develop stable habits of living, which means good work habits, people must have a stable job. The underprivileged worker is perfectly realistic when he asks, "Why should I try to save and get a little ahead in these times, when I'll be back on relief, anyhow, in a year or two?"

All this is to say that our society must offer the underprivileged worker a fair prospect, a better chance than he now has, of improving his status. It must convince him that he can secure a better life by hard work, and he can be convinced only when he sees a fair number of underprivileged *people like himself* getting reasonably secure jobs, a place to live, and a chance for promotion. I am *not* saying that society has to provide every such worker with permanent tenure and home ownership, and likewise make him a foreman in order to motivate him to work harder. But I am saying that the underprivileged worker will not improve unless he finds that there is a chance of his getting the basic social and economic rewards that I have mentioned. He must be given the realistic hope that the game is worth the candle. If he *does* change his work habits, if he does become ambitious, if he does begin to crave respectability, then industry and society must have the homes and steady jobs and education to offer him in return for this great effort.

We see that middle-class people work like beavers and have an insistent conscientiousness. They have the craving for respectability to drive them, and the hope of a better home, or better job, or higher status for their children to pull them. In order to make underprivileged people anxious to work harder and willing to bear more responsibility on the job, our industry, business, and government must convince them that they can get more out of life than they now get. This means that your system of production must expand so as to offer a larger proportion of the working class steadier jobs, good wages, and a decent place in which to live and to rear families.

From the varied histories of Pearl, Ruth, and Clark we get a stark picture of life in deprived areas, where the very struggle for survival consumes so much of one's life that higher ambitions seem almost impossible. Even in Clark's case, a momentary ambition was so quickly frustrated that he fell back into defeatism. It is this defeatism that so often has been misinterpreted as laziness or irresponsibility.

For many of the deprived, the world around them seems hostile and confusing, and such is frequently a realistic assessment. It may do us well to survey the family environment in which deprived children grow up and to contrast their values with those of the middle class.

MARITAL AND FAMILIAL INSTABILITY

Unlike the middle-class man and wife, who have interests beyond the emotional attachments of marriage—interests such as careers, social clubs and activities, and the encouragement of their children in education and careers— the lower-class man and wife tend toward a more intense emotional and sexual involvement in marriage because there is very little else for them. Such emotionality, pinning all one's hope on a single interest, however, tends to help break marriages, rather than seal them;[2] hence the larger number of

[2]Interestingly enough, one study has shown that 75 percent of lower-class women list a "good lover" as first or second in importance in defining a good husband —

separations, desertions, and remarriages among the deprived.

Contributing additionally to these breakups are the unstable roles that these married men and women are forced into. Although the lower-class man tends to narrowly define a husband as a breadwinner, and a good wife as a mother and housekeeper, and although the lower-class woman tends to look forward to such clear-cut roles,[3] economic realities tend to frustrate their achievement. The husband and father is usually incapable of meeting the needs of his family; without skills or education, he becomes dependent on welfare assistance or on the earnings of a wife who finds it easier to secure employment as a domestic or other unskilled worker. The husband and father therefore becomes an object of disrespect or even ridicule by wife, children, and community.

The deprived couple are also burdened very often by a proliferation of children. On the average statistically, the poorer the family the larger the family. The reasons are both psychological and economic. The lower-class woman is pressured to believe that bearing children is her primary reason for being, and the male, feeling weak and ineffectual in relation to the world, tends to think that fathering a string of children represents a kind of defiant demonstration that he is a real man.[4] Moreover, the family in poverty cannot always afford contraceptive devices and drugs, even if they are sufficiently informed of their uses and desirability.

The size of the family is multiplied not only by more and more children but also by the aunts and uncles, in-laws, and other relatives who constitute the "extended family" so characteristic of many lower-class subcultures. Newly married couples, unable to get housing because of discrimination or unable to afford available housing, are forced to move into the homes of relatives or friends. (In one research study, over three-fourths of the newlyweds were found to reside in such homes.[5]) Living space and privacy are thus limited, further diminishing the chances for a successful marriage and family. How much easier things are in middle-class suburbia!

These difficulties and disruptions do not go unrecognized by the children. A son who has seen his father out of work, ridiculed, and burdened by re-

---

this in spite of the fact that Kinsey noted that lower-class women fail more often to achieve sexual satisfaction in marriage than do better-educated women. (Among females with eight years of schooling or less, 28 percent had never achieved orgasm in five years of marriage, whereas the percentages were 17 for women who had attended high school and 15 for those who had attended college.) Cf. Lee Rainwater, *And the Poor Get Children* (Chicago: Quadrangle Books, Inc., 1960), p. 67, and Alfred Kinsey and others, *Sexual Behavior in the Human Female* (Philadelphia: W. B. Saunders, 1953), p. 401.

[3]Rainwater, pp. 67, 72–73.

[4]*Ibid.*, pp. 55, 85.

[5]August B. Hollingshead and Frederick C. Redlich, *Social Class and Mental Illness* (New York: Wiley, 1958), p. 127.

sponsibilities that poor education and poor financial resources cannot cope with is apt to hesitate entering marriage and undertaking family responsibilities. This reluctance is evidenced in statistics showing that among the lower classes men tend more often to marry later and to marry women much younger than themselves.[6] A daughter who has seen her mother work hard as the family provider, while her father goes unemployed or deserts the family, is apt to develop a hostile attitude toward fathers and toward males in general.[7] Many sons and daughters may have an underlying desire for marriage because society tells them it is the path to security, but many others remain unconvinced because of their own corrosive experiences of home life. The many liaisons and common-law marriages among the deprived would seem a measure of the hesitancy to enter more binding contracts. It should also be noted that, once married, a middle-class person can more easily break with his family because he can afford the legal costs; a poor man lacks the financial resources necessary for a satisfactory adjustment to family conflict.

VALUES AMONG THE DEPRIVED

Faced with the uncertainty of employment and the conflicts and instability of home life, the poor necessarily are scarcely motivated to expect much from life, and they indeed have a weak sense of the future. Middle-class people who are ambitiously oriented toward careers find it hard to understand why these people do not respond to every job opportunity, every opportunity for advancement, and every opportunity for professional development. But the poor are repeatedly exposed to experiences and situations that defeat them and force them to believe they cannot succeed. This self-image that they are failures and that opportunities are not for them must be understood by the career-oriented middle class if ever the gulf of misunderstanding is to be crossed and the poor rendered effective aid.

In discussing the poor, we should make a further distinction between certain levels of poverty, between those of the "working class" who just manage to get by in life and those of the "deprived class" who are repeatedly unemployed and thoroughly apathetic. Sociologist Joseph A. Kahl has defined a five-level class structure in America that may be useful for our purposes. To each he applies a characterizing word or phrase:[8]

---

[6]*Ibid.*, p. 126. Studies have shown that among lower-income groups 32 percent of the husbands are at least six years older than their wives.

[7]In a study of poor youth entering the Job Corps, it was found that males do not evaluate family life very favorably and that females take a similarly negative view of marriage and are not eager to become mothers or housewives.

[8]Joseph A. Kahl, *The American Class Structure* (New York: Holt, Rinehart & Winston, 1961), Chap. 7.

Upper class: *graceful living*
Upper-middle class: *career*
Lower-middle class: *respectability*
Upper-lower class: *getting by*
Lower-lower class: *apathy*

The classes that concern us here are the upper-lower and the lower-lower, both of which Kahl describes as being neither ambitious for careers nor particularly concerned about "respectability" and "superior" morality. Their attitude toward what we consider characteristic American values is interesting: they are, quite simply, indifferent to many of them (and are not, as some of the respectable middle class suppose, consciously rebellious against these values). The poor, in other words, tend to be resigned or apathetic about our traditional values and goals, which seem unattainable in their own lives and thus are to be neither believed nor disbelieved, neither supported nor opposed.

The middle-class values that the poor ignore seem to focus[9] on belief in the following ideals:

> *Achievement:* The middle class places great importance on taking risks and choosing among alternatives which, if successful, win high status and self-respect and draw respect and envy from others.
> *Hard work:* The middle class places high value on work or energetic action as the means toward achievement (the "organization man," indeed, is expected to involve himself intensely in his career or corporation and spend long hours promoting it).
> *Efficiency, practicality, and scientism:* In determining means and choosing alternative goals, the middle class is strongly influenced by what is often called the "American way of doing things"— rationally surveying every situation, making plans for improving efficiency, and employing verifiable scientific knowledge or at least so-called common sense (societal norms).
> *Progress and material comfort:* The old eighteenth and nineteenth century ideas about "progress and perfectibility" — that man can infinitely improve himself and that society is making progress toward perfection — still have a strong hold on the American middle class; and much of this progress is measured in material terms or in the improvement and wider distribution of goods and services.

The upper-lower class—roughly comprising the steadily employed unskilled and semiskilled workers and their families—fail to acknowledge or appreciate these middle-class ideals largely because of the uninspirational nature of their employment. Their work is uninteresting and mechanical; there

---

[9]For some general surveys of American ideals and values, see the following: Robin Williams, *American Society* (New York: Knopf, 1952), Chap. 11; Charles E. Ramsey and others, "Values and the Adoption of Practices," *Rural Sociology*, XXIV (1959), 35–48; Harry Schwarzweller, "Value Orientation in Educational and Occupational Choices," *Rural Sociology*, XXIV (1959), 246–56.

is little in the day-to-day routine that suggests opportunity for advancement; and, in general, things to arouse interest in one's work or career are largely absent.[10] The man of the upper-lower or working class labors simply because it is a way to make a living and avoid the hardship of long periods of unemployment; it is a "way to get by."

The deprived person's estrangement from middle-class values is far greater. The frustrations of unemployment or precarious employment, a limited sophistication that invites ridicule, as well as a succession of failures, have persuaded him, his friends, and his family that there is just no point in trying. This fatalism, resignation, or apathy does not necessarily imply that they reject the importance of achievement, hard work, and everything else that goes into the Good Life. Rather, they merely think it futile to aspire toward goals that appear not as realistic possibilities, but as fantasies.

As a substitute for achievement—which involves taking risks and seizing opportunities—the lower-lower class puts a value on security, relying on means traditionally known to them and seemingly sure and predictable. Wedded to this belief in security is the belief in barriers that cannot be breached in any event, even if they wanted or were able to hazard everything to fortune.

THE DEPRIVED CHILD AND HIS FAMILY

That deprivation tends to perpetuate itself through generations from parents to children was suggested in Chapter 1, in stating that statistically the offspring of poorly educated people tend themselves to grow up to be poorly educated. To this we have added the point that the children of broken families tend themselves to develop a dim view of marriage and home life, and the scope of the problem is suggested by the finding that approximately 50 to 60 percent of lower-class children grow up in families scarred by parental separation, desertion, or remarriage.[11]

It should be obvious by now that, in general, by the time a deprived child has reached school age his environment has constricted and handicapped him

---

[10]Kahl, pp. 205–10. See also Charles R. Walker and Robert H. Guent, *The Man on the Assembly Line* (Cambridge, Mass.: Harvard Univ. Press, 1952), and Ely Chinoy, *Automobile Workers and the American Dream* (Garden City, N.Y.: Doubleday, 1955).

[11]Kurt B. Mayer, *Class and Society* (New York: Doubleday, 1955), p. 51. Hollingshead and Redlich offer a slightly lower estimate, asserting that 41 percent of lower-class children under seventeen years of age live in homes disrupted by death, desertion, separation, or divorce (*op. cit.*, p. 124). That education and marital adjustment are related is indicated by the statistics that about 25 percent of married persons lacking a high school education end up marrying twice or more, whereas only 10 percent of college graduates remarry. Cf. Paul C. Glick and Hugh Carter, "Marriage Patterns and Educational Level," *American Sociological Review*, XXIII (June 1958), 296.

and set the pattern for failure. He has failed to learn about setting social goals or making plans, because in his home he has never heard his parents do advance planning for many things—vacations, a new home or new furniture, or their children's education. He has never acquired an understanding of how to use various social services and institutions such as libraries, legal aid, and medical clinics, because his parents never became involved in such things, even when free. He has never had the advantages of leisure-time activities normally thought to be a part of childhood—activities that would move him about and give him awareness and knowledge of his community, his school, and the wider world in which he lives. He has never been afforded the means, skills, or encouragement to gain entrance into desirable social groups that would instill in him a sense not only of social cooperation but also of intellectual competition. Finally, he has never even had the opportunity to develop the language of society: whereas "in middle-class homes children are managed largely through verbal appeals" and "parents are expert in handling disagreements with words," in lower-class families "direct action is used much more." There may even be a suspicion of verbal fluency.[12]

In an excellent summary of the literature dealing with patterns of child rearing and academic performance, sociologist Catherine S. Chilman has noted that in the low-income family parents and children develop few relations or attitudes toward one another that are conducive to good academic performance. Indeed, the whole atmosphere of the home tends to be nonintellectual, nonexploratory, and uncommunicative. She lists a comparison of educated and uneducated attitudes:[13]

EDUCATED FAMILIES	VERY POOR FAMILIES
Child given freedom within consistent limits to explore and experiment.	Limited freedom for exploration (partly explained by crowded living conditions and more dangerous environment).
Wide range of parent-guided experiences, offering visual, auditory, kinesthetic, and tactile stimulation.	Constricted lives led by parents; some fear and distrust of the unknown.
Goal commitment and belief in long-range success potential.	Fatalistic, apathetic attitude.
Gradual training for and value placed on independence.	Tendency for abrupt transition to independence; parents tend to lose control of children at an early age.
Reliance on objective evidence.	Magical and at times rigid thinking.
Much verbal communication.	Little verbal communication.

---

[12]William W. Wattenberg, "Education for the Culturally Deprived," *National Elementary Principal*, XLIV (November 1964), 17.

[13]Catherine S. Chilman, "Child Rearing and Family Relationship Patterns of the Very Poor," *Welfare in Review*, (January 1965), pp. 9–19.

| Educational and occupational success of parents; model as continuing "learners" themselves. | Tendency to educational and occupational failure; reliance on personal versus skill attributes of vocational success. |

Obviously these characteristics of educated and impoverished families are listed as general tendencies. Within any class or ethnic grouping variations will be found—so that some middle-class families will be characterized by the chilliest and most limited verbal communication or, on the other hand, some poor families will be highly compatible in freely communicating with one another. Generally speaking, however, these descriptions do reflect the observations of those who have studied patterns of child socialization and educational performance.

Educational performance, of course, involves more than the absorption of knowledge; it also refers to the socialization of the child, promoting his adjustment as an individual and as a member of social groups. Consistently in this area the poor child is again handicapped. In testing personality, Patricia Cayo Sexton presented such questions as the following to groups of low- and middle-income children: Do you get excited when things go wrong? Do you feel that classmates and friends know more than you do? Do you feel that nobody likes you? Do you have too few friends? She found that low-income children were far more likely to answer yes to these questions, thus implying minimally a lack of self-confidence and perhaps even some more serious mental disturbances. Although in most young children such insecurity could hardly be classified as psychosis or neurosis, it does tend to inhibit study and learning and the development of close relationships with one's classmates and teachers.[14]

The lack of socialization and close relationships in school probably derives from a lack of intimacy and affection in the home. Many years ago Leland H. Stott listed several characteristics of good family life that seem to promote the better adjustment of adolescent personalities—for instance:[15]

1. An affectionate and confidential relationship between each child and both his mother and his father.
2. Infrequent punishment of the children.
3. A minimum of nervousness and anxiety on the part of the father or mother.
4. Limited outside activities on the part of the mother.
5. Frequent enjoyable experiences as a family unit within the home.
6. Frequent family excursions (on visits, picnics, etc.) in which each child is an active participant.

---

[14]Patricia Cayo Sexton, *Education and Income: Inequalities of Opportunity in Our Public Schools* (New York: Viking, 1961), pp. 90–93.

[15]Leland H. Stott, "The Relation of Certain Factors in Farm Family Life to Personality Development in Adolescents," *Nebraska AES Bulletin*, No. 106 (1938). The listing given here has been adapted and abbreviated.

7. A welcoming attitude on the part of the parents toward the children's friends who visit the home.

Few of these positive relationships exist in most lower-class families. The urban poor, in particular, live in overcrowded and decaying neighborhoods, permeated by delinquency and crime, and all this has a dampening influence on any spirit of optimism and affection. People out of work or on relief rolls furthermore have little opportunity for "family excursions" and other "enjoyable experiences."

In addition to social and psychological drawbacks, most culturally deprived children have health and physical difficulties that are hardly conducive to alertness and good classroom behavior. Despite the availability of free medical services in many—though not all—regions of the United States, the poor are still less likely to be getting the treatment they need, even though their unhealthful environments may make them more subject to injury and disease. Rheumatic fever, for instance, is three times more prevalent among the lowest-income groups than among the highest. Diphtheria and tuberculosis, while almost nonexistent in high-income groups, have high rates of incidence among children of families making less than $5000 a year.[16]

Vision and hearing—so closely related to academic performance—are more frequently defective among low-income families.[17] In a recent study, Job Corpsmen were found to be usually suffering from underweight and from various dental, skin, and nutritional problems; about 80 percent had had no contact with a physician or dentist in the ten years prior to their enrollment. Indeed, only about half the lowest-income population throughout the nation have ever had a full physical examination, in contrast to about 90 percent of those in the highest-income groups.[18] All these factors suggest that as early as the primary grades, children must be given careful diagnosis in school and, if suffering from disabilities, given adequate remedial services.

DEPRIVED PARENTS AND THE PROMOTION OF EDUCATION

In pointing out that poor children receive little in the way of support and encouragement within the home, we are not implying that their parents are all indifferent to their needs or unconcerned about their progress in school. On the contrary, there is every reason to believe that usually the poor do care about the future of their children. The many protest demonstrations by urban and rural Negroes seeking to better their children's opportunities are certainly evidence that they are concerned about the education and welfare of their

---

[16]Sexton, p. 100.
[17]*Ibid.*, p. 104.
[18]*Ibid.*, pp. 101–5.

children. That many poor parents seek out extra jobs in order to better provide for their children is also indicative of a desire to give them a better life.

In seeking to understand the dynamics of behavior, however, we must differentiate between desire and ability. Although teachers may be wrong in often assuming that poor parents do not care, there must be some valid reasons why they avoid PTA meetings and other school and community activities. One reason may be one alluded to earlier—that the poor feel they cannot control their environment, that decisions are made by others, and that their task is simply to learn to adjust to these decisions. Failure to involve themselves in school activities may well reflect this overriding belief that involvement would make little difference. Another reason may be that the poor are apt to be intimidated by the formal structure of the school, since they lack the social sophistication and verbal skills essential for making demands on professionals or for manipulating the system. Inevitably they may find themselves in a position that forces them to admit their failures and thus strips them of their dignity. It is not easy for people to admit to strangers that they cannot find work, that they cannot read, or that they cannot provide for their families. Thus, the avoidance of programs that might be of help may be due not to a lack of concern or motivation, but rather to a fear of personal humiliation.

Many of the poor are also suspicious of new programs such as Operation Head Start or the Community Action Programs—at least during the initial stages of organization. Many find it difficult to believe that there are "no strings attached" or that suddenly there is a national or community interest in their dilemma. Past experience warns them that offers of assistance are frequently short lived. Among the deprived there is a feeling of resignation; high-sounding altruistic speeches and emotionally presented doctrines of brotherhood and equality can scarcely interest people who have seen the doctrines fail.

Only when the poor translate their desires into physical demonstrations, such as school boycotts and picketing, does their case receive some consideration. But even when the poor are heard out and changes are made, the people in control of the educational system who make the changes rarely put any intellectual value on what the poor desire. Rather they are simply and momentarily pressured into action by fear and anxiety. In contrast, when middle-class families want changes, they rarely have to take to the streets. Merely by meeting informally with school principals and superintendents, they exert the power to have teachers removed, library books placed on blacklists, and extra-curricular activities implemented or canceled.

Poor people fail to help their children not only by avoiding formal organizations and programs set up by the middle-class community but also by failing to assist their children informally at home. Having had a poor education themselves and lacking the skills of reading, language, and mathematics, they can hardly provide much in the way of meaningful help to their children.

They are even incapable of directing them to professional help, for they know little of libraries (or even of the process of obtaining a library card) and little about any other institutional aids and services.

All the various difficulties we have surveyed in these pages point to the conclusion suggested at the very beginning of this book: the school, rather than the family, must be relied upon to retrieve these children from their disadvantages. Every teacher, in particular, must not be indifferent to or unaware of their shortcomings. He must recognize that, regardless of age similarities, all children are not equal, but at the same time he must not assume that inabilities in cognitive areas are due to a lack of desire to succeed. The poor child, like any other child, will react to activities and curricula that are exciting. The poor child, like any other child, will respond to teachers who make it clear that they have both the desire and the ability to help him. The poor child, like the middle-class child, will be most responsive to a learning situation in which he can perceive some meaningful relation between what he is asked to do and what he views as his own goals and expectations. In the next chapter we turn for a closer look at the behavior and performance of the poor child in the setting of the school.

Suggested Readings

BERNSTEIN, BASIL. "Language and Social Class," British Journal of Sociology, XI (September 1960) 271–76.

ERICSON, MARTHA C. "Social Status and Child Rearing Practices," in Readings in Social Psychology, ed. THEODORE M. and HARTLEY NEWCOMB. New York: Holt, Rinehart & Winston, 1947.

GOTTLIEB, DAVID, and REEVES, JOHN. Adolescent Behavior in Urban Areas. New York: Free Press (a subsidiary of Crowell Collier & Macmillan, Inc.), 1963.

PETTIGREW, T. F. "Negro American Intelligence: A New Look at an Old Controversey," Journal of Negro Education, XXXIII (Winter 1964).

RIESSMAN, FRANK. The Culturally Deprived Child. New York: Harper & Row, 1962.

SHERIF, MUZAFER and CAROLYN. Problems of Youth: Transition to Adulthood in a Changing World. Chicago: Aldine, 1965.

Chapter Three: SCHOOL PERFORMANCE AND DEPRIVATION

The interlocking conditions of deprivation that cause poor parents to view the world as hostile, to resign themselves fatalistically to partial participation in the rewards of our social system, and to live in chronic ill health or physical malaise may have similar effects on their children and militate against their success in school. They may even come to school already thinking they are failures and that they can do nothing well. All this, however, is not to say that they can be left satisfied with their condition. From our own research and the reports of others, we have yet to hear of a youngster who seeks to live in poverty, alienation, or despair. We have not come in touch with a youngster coming out of poverty who has voiced a desire for a life of slums or "the hills and hollers," inferior housing, unemployment, or crime.

We have yet to meet a youngster coming from a broken home who holds the same goal for his own adult life. We have yet to hear a poor youngster say, "Man, I dig poverty — I love this social milieu."

If there is a common end or goal desired by all youth regardless of background, it is something we might call the Good Life — a life free of unemployment, poverty, social alienation, family chaos, and mental and physical illness. If these ends are labeled by some people as "middle class," then even the poor would like to be middle class. The difference is that, because of their socioeconomic background, poor youth aspire to those things that are at the entry to the Good Life, whereas the more affluent youth deal with the fringe benefits that come with a living knowledge of such a life. Middle-class youth are more precise about where and how they want to settle and about the types of adult roles they wish to play. Lower-income youngsters are less articulate and less sophisticated; the only thing they really get across is that they want something better than their current existence.

This difference in the heights to which middle- and lower-class youth aspire — the one seeking embellishments and the other merely entry into the Good Life — also separates their evaluations of schooling. Although middle-class youth may favor their juvenile or adolescent activities far above the curricular activities of school or the academic grind, they will at least fulfill the minimum academic requirements needed to stay in school. Obviously they do see, no matter how vaguely, some relation between what they are asked to do in the classroom and what they conceive as their own long-range goals. Most such youth are willing to accept the fact that if they want to enter college they must at least complete their high school studies. This is not to imply that they see the many requirements of the curriculum as meaningful or particularly stimulating. On the contrary, they may find these academic activities quite dull and, in contrast to their noncurricular involvements, hardly worth more than a mechanical investment. But in terms of their goals, they do make the investment and they do accept the system.

The same type of long-range payoff is less likely to be perceived by the deprived youngster who does not expect to go to college or who — for whatever reason — seeks an adult role that in his eyes does not require additional education. A constant theme in our research with youth who have entered the Job Corps stresses this very point. Here are youngsters whose career expectations were so much lower that they were unable to see how the formal educational process would be of benefit to them. They were unable to see, for example, a payoff relation between a knowledge of American history and the driving of a dump truck. They were unable to see where having an ability to solve complex mathematical problems would contribute to their getting something called a good job. They were also unwilling to buy the "well-rounded citizen" concept that is so often used by teachers as a means for avoiding the obvious — that, in fact, much of what goes on in the school is of little practical value to the student.

The imprecision of the poor youngster's ideas about the Good Life and the careers that provide it is not hard to understand. Unlike the middle-class youth, he has never been exposed to the better comforts of life or to parents, relatives, and other adults who have pursued careers in various educated professions. Job Corpsmen talk about having nice jobs, living in nice communities, in a nice home with a nice yard, where their children will be safe from delinquent influences. Or they may wish for "a big house on top of a hill" or a farm or a ranch. But the images are distant and vague, as if composed of a jumble of movie and television impressions or of an outsider's notions of the big landowner's life. If asked to identify specific occupational aspirations, these youth would most often answer that they were really not sure of the jobs they wanted and that their major purpose in entering the Job Corps was to get counseling and training in order to make realistic decisions. In our early research, they were asked:

> Well, let's lay aside your previous experiences and the reasons you entered the Job Corps. Now, if you could get any job you wanted, what would it be?

Many of the corpsmen admitted being puzzled by this question, but many others strained to come up with replies because they sensed that the interviewers were assuming that all young people should know at any given time what they want to do with their lives. Their replies, however, were vague — sketching the general characteristics of employment rather than noting the specifics of a specific job. These young men were extremely limited in their understanding of the scope of the occupational world and the types of jobs that could be available upon completion of their education and vocational training.

Poor youth, in any case, can have aspirations and motivations to improve themselves. Although we should recognize that they often come to school thinking they are failures, defeated thus far by their environment, we should not at the same time assume that they cannot be encouraged to think of the future and that the fatalism and apathy inherited from their parents cannot be overcome. Among Job Corpsmen — a group that has been sought out for encouragement—none of the Caucasians and only 2 percent of the Negroes indicated a feeling that "coming from the right family" was an important determinant of success. They believed that they were not stuck with their social heritage and that they could, by their own behavior, influence what roles they would play as adults. Perhaps this disregard for social heritage is slightly unrealistic from our point of view, since sociologists in recent decades "have forced us to see that socioeconomic classes in the United States are fairly static" and that the children of upper, middle, and lower classes usually retain the same relative status as adults.[1] Nevertheless, *overall* opportunities and access to the comforts of life can always be improved upon, and the important thing is that deprived youth can acquire the confidence that improvement is possible.

The questions, therefore, reduce to whether their ability to achieve measures up to their desire and whether our educational system demands certain goals and achievements that are incompatible with the goals and potential achievements of the lower class. To various aspects of these questions we now turn.

INTELLIGENCE AND SCHOOL PERFORMANCE

Commonly in many of our school systems the first measure we take of a child is his intelligence. In the past, the fact that intelligence quotients have predicted fairly accurately a child's performance in school or the grades he received convinced many people that IQ was the only factor important to understanding a student's academic performance. They were right insofar as IQ tests call for much the same kind of thinking required on subject-matter tests that we have traditionally used in grading — the kind of thinking we call "convergent," which requires a student to put items in logical or sequential order or to detect relationships, as between geometric forms, arithmetic symbols, or words. These advocates of IQ testing, however, were wrong if they felt that convergent thinking was all-important or if they denied that a certain middle-class bias was involved in the construction of the tests.

In recent years much has been made of the cultural unfairness of IQ tests. They may attempt to measure something called inborn or innate intelligence, but they can never, it seems, be free of some reliance on cultural experience. A child can be tested on his perception of squares or cubes, for instance, only if he has been culturally conditioned to the concept of squares or cubes. A lower-class child who usually engages in activities that are not particularly verbal or conceptual will therefore do poorly on IQ tests because of a lack of middle-class experiences and not necessarily because of a lower innate intelligence. (This is true at least to the degree that the tests are culturally biased, and some are very biased.) On the other hand, we must recognize that the symbolic relationships used in IQ testing, whether cultural or not, are often the very concepts one must be able to handle if one is to be successful in various occupations — particularly middle-class occupations. Thus it is important to introduce the lower-class child to experi-

---

[1]Henry A. Patin, "Class and Caste in Urban Education," *Chicago Schools Journal,* XLV (April 1964), 305.

ences that can prepare him for the thinking required in IQ tests and ultimately for the occupational roles that in modern America are more highly rewarded.

Although we can grant the great importance of convergent thinking, we must also consider another variety of thought that is largely ignored in IQ testing — namely, "divergent thinking" or creativity, which can be just as useful to society and to the individual. Unlike questions calling for convergent thinking — such as "A puppy is to a dog as a kitten is to a [   ]" — questions involving divergent thinking demand that a person let his imagination range over many possibilities and associations: he may, for instance, be called upon to try to associate the word cat with as many things and actions as he can think of—fur, claws, shiny eyes, meowing, purring, leaping, scratching, and so forth. Because we have failed to seek out this kind of imaginative or creative ability in IQ testing, we do not know for certain whether there is less of it in lower-class children than in middle-class children. We do know, however, that poor children are often required to be creative. Their bleak environment, without toys and other material devices, forces them to imagine a great deal — to imagine, for instance, that a shotgun shell or a spool is a toy soldier or that a bundle of rags is a baby doll — and to resort to originality, using whatever makeshift devices they can acquire. Middle-class youngsters, with their plastic soldiers, lifelike dolls, and other ready-made items, are under no such compulsion to indulge in fancies so extreme.

However we test mental abilities, we must never in any event routinely associate socioeconomic status and intelligence. Although the offspring of professional people are generally measured as more intelligent than the offspring of unskilled workers, there are innumerable exceptions; high IQ scores at the level of genius can be found among children of the deprived. And recent studies by the Associate U.S. Commissioner of Education for Research have shown positively that old stereotypes cannot be taken for granted: he found that, for some yet unknown reason, in large cities where figures are available dropouts have higher average IQ scores than high school graduates.[2]

CHARACTER AND SCHOOL PERFORMANCE

Joined to the question of mental ability is the question of character or personality. Is the deprived child psychologically prepared for adjustment to school situations, and are the stereotypes of delinquency really true? We might begin by quoting from an abstract of some field reports conducted many years ago by the Committee on Human Development of the University

---

[2]Marshall McLuhan and George B. Leonard, "The Class of 1989," Look, XXI (February 21, 1967), 23.

of Chicago.[3] In the study the division of classes corresponds to Joseph A. Kahl's, given on page 31:

> The values which the *upper-middle* class instill in their children are self-reliance, initiative, loyalty, good manners, and responsibility to the community. The vices against which they train their children are stealing and destruction of property, sexual immorality, bad manners, and carelessness in dress and speech.
>
> In the upper-middle class ... one is expected to be honest toward all people; and honest in matters of property, of truth telling, and of keeping promises. In the lower class, honesty is limited to dealings within the family and within a small neighborhood group. The average lower-class person does not feel compelled to tell the truth to everybody, to be careful of the property of everyone, or to keep his promises to everyone.
>
> The *lower-middle* and *upper-lower* classes are very much alike in their values. They stress respectability, thrift, loyalty, responsibility to family and church, and fidelity in marriage. . . . The majority accept school simply as a means of getting children ready for adulthood. Education, for them, is necessary for individual vocational success. The socially mobile minority of this group — those who are trying to "improve their station in life"— look on college as a means for getting their children ahead in the world, but the majority think of high-school graduation as the highest educational goal. . . .
>
> The *lower-lower* class are thought to be immoral, by those above them on the social scale. The members of this class are arrested more frequently than those of any other group. Their violations of the code of sexual morality are, if not more frequent, at least more widely known and more flagrant than those of other groups. On the other hand, there are some thoroughly respectable families in this social group who, because of being "foreigners" or because of poverty, are placed in the lowest class.
>
> The principal values held by the lower-lower class center about food, leisure, and family solidarity. The moral virtues of honesty, responsibility, and loyalty are restricted to a small sphere of action that includes the family and a few neighbors or friends.
>
> It seems probable that at least some of the moral ideals held up to children of the lower-lower class are different from those taught to children in the other classes. Stealing is more apt to be overlooked or condoned. Church influence is absent or weak. The moral teaching of the school is not so strongly reinforced by the home, and children of this class tend to drop out of school at an earlier age than children of other social classes. Lower-class children are taught to fight. They experience more open exhibition of aggression in their homes, where the father may beat the mother, the children are whipped frequently, and the child's own aggressive impulses are not much restrained by his parents.
>
> Similarly, lower-class children suffer less restraint on sex play and sex exploration than do middle-class children.
>
> As a generalization it might be said that lower-class children have fewer and less rigid controls on the free play of their impulses, while middle-class children are made to inhibit their impulses through the watchfulness of their

---

[3]Robert J. Havighurst and Dorothy Neubauer, "Community Factors in Relation to Character Formation," in *Adolescent Character and Personality*, eds. Robert J. Havighurst and Hilda Taba (New York: Wiley, 1949), pp. 32–34.

parents and the ever-present question in their own minds, "What will people think?"

Lower-class life in Prairie City[4] differs in one important way from lower-class life in a metropolis. The great city presents the disturbing phenomenon of "disorganized areas" in which, from the middle-class viewpoint, social values have gone awry. In these areas it is normal for a child to steal, to lie to the authorities, and to be sexually delinquent. In fact, delinquency is normal, and only those children who deviate from the normal have a chance of adopting middle-class values. This phenomenon of a "delinquency culture" is possible because of the geographical fragmentation of the city, which forces thousands of lower-class people to live together, with their own schools and places of recreation, and which effectively prevents their children from having contact with children from other social classes.

In Prairie City there is very little segregation by social class, and there is no "disorganized area."... Thus [children of the lower-lower class] are exposed in the school and on the playground to middle-class influences among their own age group. There are not delinquent groups in Prairie City, though of course some groups of young people have lower reputations than others.

Other studies have tended to confirm the conclusions drawn by the researchers at the University of Chicago. William W. Wattenberg, director of the Delinquency Control Training Center at Wayne State University, has noted that deprived youth are inclined "toward greater open display of aggressiveness" and "open expression of anger." He cautions, however, that newspaper headlines tend to "leave a false impression of the volume of disorder" and to ignore that many lower-class children want to regard their teachers as "protectors" against unruliness, their own apparently as well as that of others.[5] They would prefer an absence of violence, at least in school. Alfred Kinsey, of course, gave evidence that social class and sexual activity are related and that low-income youth tend to engage in sexual intercourse at earlier ages. On the other hand, he also found that those youth who were able to build up resistance against their environment and to plan for an education were apt to adopt the more moderate sexual mores of the higher social class to which they were aspiring.

Robert J. Havighurst, who helped direct the study of "Prairie City," later noted that by the very nature of their environment deprived youth are not impelled to achieve maturity in their social relations, at least from the middle-class point of view.[6] Compared to the more formally organized clubs

---

[4]Prairie City was the fictitious name used to conceal the identity of the small Midwestern city that was studied by researchers Havighurst, Taba, and others of the University of Chicago.

[5]William W. Wattenberg, "Education for the Culturally Deprived," *National Elementary Principal*, XLIV (November 1964), 18.

[6]Robert J. Havighurst, *Human Development and Education* (New York: Longmans, Green, 1953).

and smooth-working cliques of middle-class youth, the gangs of deprived youth seem to require fewer social skills. There is less of a need to be flexible and to adapt one's behavior to a variety of people and situations. These gangs seem also to tend toward violence and "wars" (although the violence is usually exaggerated in the popular mind), and thus physical prowess is regarded as a criterion of manhood among lower-class youth. All boys in our culture, Havighurst suggests, have difficulty achieving masculinity because they have few masculine models to imitate — their fathers usually being around less than their mothers, and their teachers being almost always women. Deprived youth, however, with their gangs and physically oriented values, tend to acquire models among their older peers and maybe even to exaggerate their attempts at virility.

Perhaps to their advantage, lower-class youth do seem to have it easier achieving emotional independence from their parents. Middle-class parents tend to be protective and to offer more guidance in the selection of occupations and marriage partners. To the extent that this guidance or support becomes interference, middle-class youth have a difficult time freeing themselves from parental control and psychological dependence. Lower-class parents, on the other hand, are more relaxed and tend to have less contact with their children. The children are thus put on their own earlier and more completely. What they lose under these conditions is any encouragement to "get ahead," to be successful in life; they are less apt to internalize this ethic.

With little encouragement from their parents and few opportunities to participate in community organizations or civic-oriented activities, deprived youth also seem rarely to achieve "civic competence," according to Havighurst. Although the recent development of special projects for slum youth indicates that they can indeed adjust to community responsibilities, most of them hear no talk about politics or social responsibilities and never engage in such talk, let alone action. Those Negro youth who participate in civil-rights movements, for instance, still constitute a very small percentage of the total Negro youth among the deprived.

Out of all this discussion of the character and personality of deprived youngsters, we should draw special attention to two things. First, quite obviously all judgments are made in terms of middle-class values or expectations; that is, a child will be judged on the degree of his conformity to the middle-class ideal. It may be noted, for instance, how often a certain qualifier was thrown into statements: persons of the lower class did not measure up to a particular standard "from the middle-class point of view" or in the judgment of "those above them on the social scale." Now, few people would object to such a criterion. Adhering to middle-class values is socially and materially rewarding in our culture. What is interesting is the implications. People in a position to apply judgments — teachers, for instance — will ordinarily be favorably disposed toward youth with middle-class backgrounds because these youth usually have adopted rather naturally the expected behavior patterns of honesty, loyalty, responsibility, and so forth. Indeed, as Nora L. Weckler discovered in studying "Prairie City," not only do most middle-class children "adopt the appropriate behavior patterns with comparative ease" but also "their teachers and other school personnel are predisposed in their favor because of the influential social status of the families of these children."[7] Lower-class children did not receive this blessing. However, Weckler went on to report that teachers were not necessarily prejudiced against lower-class children. Those children who exerted extra effort, won out over their depressing environments, and succeeded in achieving middle-class goals in school were given a high rating for character, generally equal to that given to children of middle-class backgrounds. Although most lower-class children did acquire a low reputation, their actual behavior — not their stereotyped background — was the basis for judgment. (This generalization, however, must be severely modified for certain ethnic groups — Negroes, Mexicans, and Puerto Ricans — whose "visible" disadvantage can elicit the prejudices of many white teachers, whether or not the children's behavior meets other middle-class standards.)

The second point we need to emphasize is one allied with the first: deprived youth cannot be wholly stereotyped. In spite of the environmental influences that tend to degrade their character (from the middle-class viewpoint), some of them do succeed through efforts unknown to middle-class youth, whose path is so much easier. In Weckler's words, "those lower-class youths who are successful in conforming to middle-class goals, as shown in their relatively high school achievement and high character reputation, are exerting greater effort to attain these goals than are middle- and upper-class youth."[8] The problem is that their numbers are small, and the solution is to find ways of eliciting from more youth this latent ability to take responsibility and make the effort. In other words, the stereotype of lower-class behavior is not engrained irrevocably in the individuals of that class.

HOME ENVIRONMENT AND SCHOOL PERFORMANCE

We have earlier stated and implied that children from deprived homes do not get basically oriented to education or to intellectual things in general. Their families do not set an example of reading habits or even discussion. Questions are neither encouraged nor answered. Verbal fluency is poor. Plan-

[7]Nora L. Weckler, "Social Class and School Adjustment in Relation to Character Reputation," in *Adolescent Character and Personality*, eds. Robert J. Havighurst and Hilda Taba (New York: Wiley, 1949), p. 53.
[8]*Ibid.*, pp. 54-55.

ning is feeble or nonexistent. And the struggle to "get by" develops conditions of fatigue and lassitude. In general, parents do not stress the values of education, and even if they do so verbally, their children may be unable to see the significance of the values and thus unable to accept them.

In addition to these general handicaps, we must interpolate here some more immediate, daily constrictions that surround the deprived child. He is discouraged from doing homework not only because of lack of parental support and aid but also because of poor lighting, crowded rooms, and a peer culture that depreciates homework. Whereas a middle-class child has a place to go that is relatively quiet for his homework, the deprived child is crowded among many siblings of different ages, all in two or three rooms; a bare light bulb hangs from the ceiling; and tired parents do not enforce quiet, much less homework. Quite obviously, all these factors put the child into a poor competitive position in school and militate against his keeping up with day-to-day classroom activities. This daily lag eventually becomes a lag of months and years.

PEER RELATIONSHIPS AND SCHOOL PERFORMANCE

The values held by any group of children — or "peers"— obviously influence what they will strive for and, more specifically in our case, how they will behave in school. All boys and girls — and adults for that matter — are interested in being looked up to and considered important by those they associate with. If their peers value academic achievement, they will strive harder scholastically. If their peers applaud the athletic hero, they will compete more strongly on the field than in the classroom. If their peers value physical prowess in boys or sex appeal in girls, they will be influenced to strive for these distinctions. As it happens, adolescent groups in most schools do not value academic achievement nearly so much as these other distinctions. As sociologist James S. Coleman discovered in studying ten northern Illinois schools of various types,

> . . . in all of them, academic achievement did not count for as much as other activities. In every school the boy named as best athlete and the boy named as most popular with girls was far more often mentioned as a member of the leading crowd, and as someone "to be like" than was the boy named as the best student. And the girl named as best dressed, and the one named as most popular with boys, was in every school far more often mentioned as being in the leading crowd and as someone "to be like" than was the girl named as the best student.
> The relative unimportance of academic achievement . . . suggests that these adolescent subcultures are generally deterrents to academic achievement. In other words, in these societies of adolescents those who come to be seen as "intellectuals" and who come to think so of themselves are not really those of

highest intelligence but are only the ones who are willing to work hard at a relatively unrewarded activity.[9]

We have already suggested that deprived youth lack intellectual interests; they do not sit around discussing subject matter, grades, or probably even teachers. But neither, apparently, do middle-class youth — if we accept the findings of Coleman and other researchers who have borne him out. What Coleman points out, however, is that middle-class youth will achieve scholastically in some measure in spite of the fact that immediate rewards are lacking. Perhaps not as a group, but "as *individuals*," he says, middle-class adolescents do "highly prize good grades," because good grades will get them into a good college, which both they and their parents look forward to. To say that popularity does not go with good grades merely means that scholastic achievement "does not give a boy or girl status in the eyes of his fellows."[10] In other words, the popular middle-class student may not study as hard as he might; he may divert considerable attention to athletics, social activities, and the like, which win him status among his peers; but he will also reserve some measure of personal commitment to his long-range educational goal.

Still another qualifier must be stated. Although in no school studied by Coleman did academic achievement rate as the *highest* criterion for popularity, it did come in second or third in importance in some schools (behind athletic accomplishment, leadership in extracurricular activities, or good looks). Most significantly, the rating given academic achievement was consistently higher in middle-class schools than in lower-class schools. In other words, in schools with a predominance of students whose parents were middle-class and educated, academic achievement was viewed with more favor than it was in schools with students largely of a working-class background.

In every school the "leading-crowd" or "elite" consists of those adolescents whom the great majority of students respect and try to imitate. If the school is predominantly middle-class, the leading crowd mirrors middle-class characteristics and may even magnify or accentuate these characteristics. If the school is predominantly lower-class, the leading crowd will exemplify lower-class characteristics. Therefore, says Coleman, "a working-class boy or girl will be most left out in an upper-middle-class school, least so in a school with few middle-class students."[11]

The ways in which all this works against the deprived child should be obvious. If his peers in school are predominantly of his own class, they actu-

---

[9]Reprinted from "The Adolescent Subculture and Academic Achievement" by James S. Coleman, from *The American Journal of Sociology*, LXV (January 1960), 134.

[10]James S. Coleman, *The Adolescent Society*. New York: Free Press (a subsidiary of Crowell Collier & Macmillan, Inc.), 1961, p. 80.

[11]*Ibid.*, p. 109.

ally discourage any aspirations he may have for middle-class status. Their approval for candidacy to the leading crowd depends on his retaining, at least overtly, his lower-class outlook and behavior. If, on the other hand, he goes to a predominantly middle-class school, his advantages and disadvantages are rather mixed. He may be exposed to middle-class influences (that would be virtually absent in a lower-class school), but he will find it tough going if he tries to find favor among his peers and acceptance into the leading crowd.

In either case, pressure is on him to drop out of school when he is legally able to. In a lower-class school, there are few educational aspirations anyway, even among parents of his peers. In middle-class schools, he is considered an outsider. No person — adult or child — cares to remain in an organization in which he gets few rewards and little respect from his peers. His teachers may encourage him to bear along for the moment, impressing upon him the dire consequences of dropping out. But if he is currently feeling frustration and suffering from ostracism, pretty pictures of the very distant future are not likely to have much effect on him.

Before leaving the subject of peer cultures, we must offer a few other observations. In a study of youth in Colorado, for instance, it was found that both middle- and lower-class students showed a preference for clubs or organizations that were largely or entirely "social," in which one learned how to get along with other people. Unlike middle-class boys, however, lower-class boys also showed an interest in clubs that taught one such things as carpentry, home remodeling, and electrical work.[12] Perhaps this finding reinforces our earlier contention that deprived youth are more apt to take an interest in education if they can see in it some immediate practical value. Perhaps it also indicates the usefulness of clublike associations in educating these youth.

A more important observation is related to the question of discrimination by class or ethnic background. In elementary school, children discriminate little on the basis of class or color — at least in their choice of playmates. In studies made in Philadelphia, Helen G. Trager and Marian Radke found that although children coming from a home prejudiced against a minority group had already absorbed this prejudice by the time they entered school, they proceeded to have friendly associations with members of the minority group anyway.[13] They did show their prejudice occasionally in word and action — and children can be thoughtlessly vicious in applying nicknames — but generally a kind of equalitarian attitude prevailed. Of course, even this sort of ambivalent prejudice can subtly scar the minority child

---

[12]Charles E. Ramsey and Manuel Alers, "A Study of Youth from Low Status Families" (unpublished manuscript, 1967).

[13]Helen G. Trager and Marian Radke, "Early Childhood Airs Its Views," Educational Leadership, V (1947), 16–24.

and make him feel somehow that he is inferior. And if a poor child has physical infirmities (bad eyes, bad teeth, weak limbs, etc.) as a result of being deprived of medical services, he may become the object of more decided ridicule and discrimination.

Junior high school presents a transitional stage, when social consciousness is becoming more apparent. Some dating begins, particularly on the part of girls (who reach sexual maturation earlier), and if their parents foster social differentiation, the choice of dates may be based on status criteria.

As we move into the high school years, we find conditions becoming more complicated. Racial prejudice may become more pronounced — as pronounced as it is among the parents of the children. But discrimination not involving race is harder to analyze. If an adolescent attends a school in which almost all his peers are of the same class, there is little problem — if one considers only the discrimination among peers within that school. In middle-class schools, however, the minority of lower-class adolescents are effectively excluded from gaining access to the leading crowd. This does not necessarily mean, according to Coleman, that an adolescent fails in popularity or becomes an "outsider" simply because of class — because his parents are uneducated or lack a privileged position in the community. Students do not ordinarily look at his background and then rate him. Rather, it seems that the influence of his background is usually more indirect. He has not acquired the superior training or material advantages (such as money for cars, clothes, and dates) that middle-class parents give their children, nor has he absorbed the middle-class outlook that his more privileged peers have come to value. Thus, few lower-class children make it among a predominantly middle-class group, but the reason is usually not direct discrimination by class.[14]

POOR GRADES AND DROPOUTS

The rewards that encourage any person to remain in an organization involve not only his formal relations with colleagues or peers but also his formal attainments. In school, this means that a child may possibly be influenced to drop out if he finds no fellowship among his peers nor any reasonable opportunity to join clubs or achieve in sports — everything that a peer culture finds enjoyable. But, more formally, it means that he may not find even the rewards that are officially distributed by the school. His grades, if poor, may be decisive in discouraging him from continuing on an educational course that does not appear fruitful.

Although grades have come under attack by educators in recent years,

---

[14]In addition to Coleman, pp. 103–10, see Robert J. Havighurst and others, *Growing Up in River City* (New York: Wiley, 1962), Chap. 4, which presents a slightly different view.

principally on the grounds that they inaccurately reflect academic achievement and intellectual ability, there is no question of their social importance in the present system of things. On the basis of grades, people are hired or rejected from employment, admitted to or rejected by colleges, and generally given or denied many of the breaks of life. Thus, if a student does not get grades sufficiently high to merit some respect, he has a poor chance of fitting into our affluent society.

Deprived youth have poor chances of fitting in. Although exceptions have been found, most lower-class children do less well in grades than middle-class children. In a study of high school students, for instance, August deB. Hollingshead found that almost all the failing grades were given to lower-class students and most of the top marks were given to middle- and upper-class students.[15] (This distribution is especially interesting when one considers that in Coleman's adolescent society no prestige is generally attached to getting good grades; good marks thus seemingly come to middle-class youth as a matter of course.)

However poor his grades, the deprived child is much better off if he accepts them (or tries to better them) than if he backs off from them and drops out of school. Employers and colleges naturally attach even more importance to diplomas than to grades. Though perhaps feeling initially relieved and unburdened, the dropout soon finds out that worthwhile jobs are just not available to him. Again, as in grades, we find that lower-class children have the poorest record: at least three times as many lower-class youth drop out of school as do youth of other classes.[16] And, even more significant, poor grades almost always are a prelude to dropping out.

Suggested Readings

AUSUBEL, DAVID P. "A Teaching Strategy for Culturally Deprived Pupils: Cognitive and Motivational Considerations," *School Review*, LXXI (Winter 1963), 454–63.
COLEMAN, JAMES S. *The Adolescent Society*. New York: Free Press (a subsidiary of Crowell Collier & Macmillan, Inc.), 1961.
———. "The Adolescent Subculture and Academic Achievement," in *Readings in the Social Psychology of Education*, eds. W. W. CHARTERS and N. L. GAGE. Boston: Allyn & Bacon, 1963. Reprinted from *American Journal of Sociology*, LXV (January 1960), 337–47.
GOTTLIEB, DAVID, and TENHOUTEN, WARREN D. "Racial Composition and the Social Systems of Three High Schools," *Journal of Marriage and the Family*, XXVII (May 1965), 204–12.
HERRIOT, ROBERT E., and ST. JOHN, NANCY A. *Social Class and the Urban School*. New York: Wiley, 1966.

---

[15]August deB. Hollingshead, *Elmtown's Youth* (New York: Wiley, 1949), Chap. 8.

[16]Havighurst and others, *Growing Up in River City*, Chap. 5. See also Hollingshead, *Elmtown's Youth*.

KATZ, IRWIN. "Review of Evidence Relating to Effects of Desegregation on the Intellectual Performance of Negroes," *American Psychologist*, XIX (June 1964), 381–99.

PASSOW, A. HARRY (ed.). *Education in Depressed Areas*. New York: Teachers College, 1963.

Chapter Four: DEPRIVATION IN THE CLASSROOM AND THE SCHOOL

Deprivation, we have shown, is a complex of many variables — poverty, lack of educational influence, discrimination by class and race, ill health, and so forth — and the child experiences this deprivation not only in the home but also among his associates in and out of school. Although we have already touched on his inadequate readiness for schooling — in IQ testing and grading — and on his unfavorable relations with his peers, we must turn to his teachers and to the curricular and institutional setting of the school for still additional disadvantages.

With the growth in our understanding of deprived students there has come the almost universal recognition that teaching methods, teacher attitudes, and school functions have not in the past been quite appropriate for the disadvantaged child. Curricula and methods — insofar as they encourage competition, emphasize academic rigor, and draw upon middle-class experiences — have favored the middle-class student; even recent innovations such as the new math, the new social studies, and the new English have been more largely aimed at middle- or upper-class children or at least at the progressive teacher found more often in middle-class schools. Such programs are reasonably successful and therefore needed, and to give them up and promote new policies merely for the sake of assuring equal competition for the deprived child would be wrong — creating, as it might, even more serious problems overall. The question, therefore, is not one of complete and general change, but of special adjustments and changes for the deprived child in particular.

In order to make such adjustments, of course, we must first look at the present state of things.

THE ATTITUDES OF TEACHERS

In research comparing the value orientations of people in various occupations, teachers have consistently ranked very high in their social concern and their respect for other human beings. Indeed, they have often ranked second only to social workers. Thus one could surmise that they would make a reasonably strong effort to understand the deprived students in their classrooms, to try to reach them in spite of their lack of motivation and interest in learning. The evidence is otherwise. Although teachers may start with high hopes and great concern, they, like any other human beings, can be defeated by repeated frustrations in trying to overcome deprivation — in much the same fashion that deprived people themselves ultimately become resigned and apathetic. Thus the blame is generally not on the individual teachers, but on the system.

Although exact figures are not available, it is known that the rate of teacher turnover is very high in schools serving disadvantaged children. Even those teachers who stay on express decreasing satisfaction with their jobs as the years wear on.[1] Some say they feel inadequate for the kind of teaching required; some stress problems of discipline and negative behavior or of excessively large classes. Some reveal an obvious lack of understanding and acceptance of disadvantaged children, but even if they try to understand, they tend to apply blanket criticisms to deprived children — sometimes legitimately, sometimes not. Research in the Detroit inner city, for instance, piled up this list of accusations made by teachers against deprived students:[2]

---

[1]See David Gottlieb, "Teaching and Students: The Views of Negro and White Teachers," *Sociology of Education*, XXXVII (Summer 1964), 345–53; and Patrick J. Groff, "Dissatisfactions in Teaching the CD Child," *Phi Delta Kappan*, XLV (November 1963).

[2]Research Committee of the Coordinating Council on Human Relations, Detroit, "The Challenge to Education in the Multi-Problem Neighborhoods" (mimeographed report, Detroit, April 20, 1961).

1. They score low on IQ and other tests.
2. They read and speak poorly and perform below grade level on other tasks.
3. They are not motivated toward the academic goals teachers hold, such as completing high school, going to college, and the like.
4. They are not well disciplined or taught good manners in their homes.
5. They are not clean.
6. They are not interested in school or the future.
7. They cannot or will not learn.
8. They tend toward toughness, violence, listlessness, dishonesty, a perverted sense of humor, and sexual license.

Some of these charges might be supported by even the most sympathetic and well-meaning person. A dirty, malodorous child could turn away any teacher who might otherwise want to give attention. Some of the charges, however, represent merely a cultural bias against those who do not aspire to higher education or respectable middle-class manners. It is one thing to recognize that these problems exist through no inherent fault of the child, and another thing to oppose him because he lacks one's own values.

A teacher's own background seems to have a great deal to do with his attitude toward deprived children. If he himself has risen out of a lower-class environment, he is much more apt to take an understanding view of things. In a study of elementary teachers in a Midwestern inner-city community, for instance, Negro teachers generally had a much lower socioeconomic background than white teachers and, correspondingly, took a more charitable view of their disadvantaged children. The middle-class white who had always been middle class was ill-prepared for the conditions in which he found himself:[3]

> The individual whose own educational experience included being part of a middle class culture where children were "well behaved" and sophisticated in the handling of educational tasks, and whose parents played an active role in the school and saw to it that their children did their school work, no doubt experiences a feeling of "cultural shock" when placed in the setting of the inner city school. When such an individual's expectations are not modified by what is taught in schools of education, there is little reason to believe that they will be realistic. The fact that Negro teachers are more likely than white teachers to come from backgrounds similar to those of the children of the inner city probably tends to make them more realistic in their expectations, and hence less likely to be dissatisfied with their current teaching roles.
>
> Some empirical evidence to support [this] observation . . . comes from responses to a question dealing with changes that these teachers feel should be made in current training of school teachers. . . . Almost two thirds of the white teachers suggest revisions that would make the training program more realistic. Among the Negro teachers there is a greater dispersion of responses, with only 26% of the group expressing a need for more realistic types of educational prep-

---

[3]Gottlieb, pp. 349–53 passim.

aration. . . . The Negro teachers are more likely than the white to see a need for "greater selectivity" of education majors and for more thorough training in substantive areas such as reading and arithmetic. . . .

There are, of course, other possible explanations of the differences in satisfaction. There may be a greater sympathy with the Negro child and his problems on the part of the Negro teacher. . . . Negro teachers tend to emphasize problems related to the physical setting of the school while white teachers are more likely to stress problems pertaining to the shortcomings of the students. . . . [For instance, as] reasons for job dissatisfaction . . . the two items most frequently mentioned by white teachers are "lack of parental interest" and "student behavior or discipline problems." Although some Negro teachers do express concern over these same problems, they tend to place the greater emphasis on factors such as "lack of proper equipment" and "overcrowded conditions.". . . [Thus] in the case of the Negro teachers . . . the tendency is toward holding the system responsible for problems on the job and not this particular group of children. . . .

Each teacher was given a list containing thirty-three adjectives and asked to check those adjectives which came closest to describing the outstanding characteristics of the children with whom she was working. . . . The five items that are most frequently selected by white teachers in order of frequency are: "Talkative," "Lazy," "Fun Loving," "High Strung," and "Rebellious." The five items most frequently selected by Negro teachers in order of frequency are: "Fun Loving," "Happy," "Cooperative," "Energetic," and "Ambitious." The only item mentioned among the top five by both groups of teachers is "Fun Loving.". . . Most teachers are in agreement that these children do not possess those qualities usually associated with middle class children. They are not "Cultured," "Dominant," "Forceful," "Poised," "Witty," or "Sophisticated."

Generally white teachers tend to avoid those adjectives which reflect stability and the types of qualities one would desire of children in the formal classroom setting. Negro teachers on the other hand select items which seem to be universal attributes of children (i.e., energetic, fun loving, and happy) in addition to those which appear to go hand-in-hand with a successful learning experience (i.e., ambitious and cooperative).

Again, it would appear that the Negro teachers are less critical and less pessimistic in their evaluations of these students than the white, probably because many of them have themselves come from backgrounds similar to that of their students and yet have managed to overcome social barriers to attain positions of responsibility and status.

Teachers who have risen out of the lower class may have a better understanding of the conditions in which their children live and learn (or fail to learn), but one must not automatically assume that such understanding necessarily by itself assures that they will teach effectively in the classroom. Bruce R. Joyce has noted that "a teacher who has known poverty may deliberately seek the education of poor children but may make the mistake of being too hard on them in an effort to drive them into seeking status themselves."[4] Marvin A. Brottman has similarly noted, "It may be that

---

[4] Bruce R. Joyce and Berj Harootunian, *The Structure of Teaching* (Chicago: Science Resarch Associates, 1967), p. 215.

when an individual [from the lower class] has become a teacher with its attendant high status, he might not care to be reminded of his class origin. His origin might be denied by insisting on perfection in class or by being more middle class in expectations of students than a teacher from a middle-class environment."[5] There are even instances of persons trying to avoid teaching in a deprived neighborhood because it reminds them too much of the environment that they entered teaching to escape. (Again, however, deprivation sets up its barriers against escape, for, whether or not he wants it, "opportunities for placement in a different kind of school setting are unlikely for the Negro teacher."[6])

Problems of Discipline

Discipline has been listed by middle-class teachers as one of their major problems, and if it seems less of a problem to teachers out of the lower class, it is still not unknown to them. In the familiar "blackboard jungle," such as the schools coded "600" in the slums of New York City, some of the students are extremely difficult to control in the classroom, but control is a problem in any disadvantaged school, though it may be less subject to sensationalism and violence.

Part of the reason is that, unlike middle-class youth who have learned to channel their aggressions into social and economic competition, lower-class youth tend to find an outlet for their aggressions in physical demonstration — talking, fidgeting, rebelling, and uneasily killing time.[7] Such aggression tends occasionally to elicit corresponding aggression from the teacher — resistance meeting resistance. Too often the teacher's reaction merely intensifies the student's aggression and, in effect, produces part of the discipline problem.

One difficulty is that physical communication is a far greater part of the everyday pattern of life among the deprived, and this extends to punishment. In the home, direct physical action is used more than psychological punishment (such as withholding love or approval or delivering verbal appeals), and to this action the parents generally add emotional anger, which is not the best model of behavior to present to children who are being punished for the very reasons of aggression. As psychologist Frank Reissman has further pointed out, "there seems to be considerable ambivalence toward aggression in this [deprived] culture. While it is rejected as a form of response

---

[5]Marvin A. Brottman, "Dimensions of the Problem of the Disadvantaged Pupil," in *Teaching the Culturally Disadvantaged Pupil*, eds. John M. Beck and Richard W. Saxe (Springfield, Ill.: Charles C Thomas, 1965), p. 23.

[6]Gottlieb, p. 350.

[7]Allison Davis, *Social-Class Influences upon Learning* (Cambridge, Mass.: Harvard Univ. Press, 1950), pp. 34–35.

to the parents and family, it is expected that the child will stand up for him-self, and fight if necessary, in the outer environment."[8]

All this puts the teacher in a disagreeable position. Most psychologists would agree, in any event, that punishment is not generally effective in deterring or eliminating aggressive behavior — and may eventually aggra-vate this behavior[9]— but even if the teacher should try to soft-pedal his tendency to punish, he is still seen by his students as the outsider or part of the "outer environment" that their culture tells them requires no deference or respect.

The teacher might possibly return this disrespect in kind. In schools with a mixture of middle- and lower-class children, for instance, Hollings-head found a tendency to overlook the occasional rebellions of middle-class students; they were far less often sent to the "detention room," and even when they were, they were forgiven their trespasses much more easily. The attitude toward lower-class youth was far more rigid. A reprieve from a sentence to the detention room was rarely granted in the way it often was for children of higher status.[10]

In Hollingshead's school, truancy among lower-class youth was treated with what may seem like paradoxical leniency. Apparently, however, the school administrator winked at such truancy merely out of recognition that it was a sign of gradual withdrawal and eventual dropping out. In recent years the motivations for such leniency have become much more complicated. In a study of a large Western city, it was found that although deprived children were truant a good deal of the time, everyone was somewhat satis-fied if they adhered to a certain minimum rate of attendance. The children themselves condescended to attend school just the exact number of days required to qualify their parents for "aid to dependent children," thus satis-fying themselves and their parents. The principal of the school was reasonably content if the children attended enough to keep the school qualified for the full amount of state aid (which is always based on the average daily attendance of students); such a requirement constrained him to withhold putting pressure on the students for fear they would drop out altogether. The social workers were satisfied to keep quiet about the whole matter, for they knew that any publicity about the rate of truancy might raise public objections to the aid to dependent families, thus perhaps canceling this aid that social workers feel is absolutely necessary for maintaining minimum standards of diet, housing, and clothing. In today's world, therefore, a variety

---

[8]Frank Riessman, *The Culturally Deprived Child* (New York: Harper & Row, 1962), p. 40.

[9]*Ibid.*, p. 39.

[10]August deB. Hollingshead, *Elmtown's Youth* (New York: Wiley, 1949), Chap. 8.

of people have a vested interest in allowing sporadic attendance on the part of deprived students.

Parent-teacher conferences on matters of discipline seem to be frustrated on every hand. The parents themselves are reluctant to become involved. As we noted in Chapter 2, they are somewhat frightened by the formality and sophistication of the academic setting and its representatives and feel ill-equipped to pit themselves against teachers or even to collaborate with them; they are unwilling to submit themselves to the scrutiny that would expose their inadequacies and failures. For his part, the middle-class teacher who lacks awareness or understanding of their problems is apt to write them off as indifferent, anti-intellectual, unconcerned about their children's development. If they do not respond to his notes or requested appointments, he thinks, what else can it be but indifference? Of course, even if he is understanding, his understanding may include the recognition that such parents may react to bad news about their children by severely punishing them physically or raising some other kind of storm — hardly a proper solution to the socialization of children in this day and age.

Teachers do not always look favorably on conferences with parents in any case. Even with middle-class parents, they fear being put on the defensive, trying to prove that the children are at fault while parrying the possible charge that they themselves are to blame. With lower-class parents, teachers may feel that they have more of an upper hand as far as sophistication is concerned, but the element of antagonism can still be unnerving. Furthermore, many teachers regard themselves as experts and professionals and the parents as mere laymen and thus feel that parental aid and influence are at best distractions.

Problems of Instruction

In any occupation, self-respect and the respect of others come with the successful performance of one's tasks — in teaching, with the successful development of the capabilities and interests of one's students. Teachers feel especially rewarded if their children are "interested in attending and working hard in the school, and are trained at home in such a way that they are bright and quick at school work."[11] This, of course, generally means working in a middle- or upper-class school, and indeed almost universally teachers consider it a mark of advancement or promotion if they can make their way into such a school; at the least, they consider themselves lucky. Prestige and self-respect, however, are not the only factors. Nationwide, salary schedules in suburban schools are almost always higher (in 1966, from 2.8 percent

---

[11]Howard S. Becker, "Social-Class Variations in the Teacher-Pupil Relationship," *Journal of Educational Sociology*, XXV (April 1952), 453.

higher for beginners to 10.6 percent higher for teachers with doctorates[12])
than they are in urban systems; and suburban schools are where one finds
the "bright and quick" middle-class children. Thus financially teachers are
attracted away from lower-class children and into systems offering all the
more pleasant rewards.

Until recently, before the influx of federal funds, deprived children had
therefore not even begun to get the best attention or the best, most experi-
enced teachers. Although young teachers have frequently entered education
with a certain missionary zeal and dedication to the ideal of "helping
children," including deprived children, the frustrations of teaching in disadvantaged schools with large enrollments and inadequate money — added
to the general professional burdens of clerical duties, committee meetings,
parent conferences, and the like — have tended to drive these teachers off
into more congenial working environments, just at the moment that they
may have been gathering some experience in instructing deprived youngsters. Even today, federal funds have yet to overcome this problem of
constant teacher turnover.

The day-to-day problems of teaching deprived children can be quite per-
plexing. Initially, teachers in the higher grades receive children who have
fallen behind in lower grades and come ill-prepared for advanced instruction.
Then each day they come to class having failed to do the homework that
would make the teacher's job much easier. If the teacher has a mixture of
middle- and lower-class students in his classroom, his problems are com-
pounded, for how does one decide how to conduct lessons when some
students have done their homework and others have not? Heterogeneity is the
curse of any classroom at any level in the educational institution.

When there is a mixture of students, moreover, almost inevitably the
teacher tends to interact oftener with the more responsive students, thus
giving middle-class students more attention even though they may possibly
need it less. If a portion of these students are college-preparatory, the teacher
who is oriented toward subject matter can be expected to show an even
greater degree of interest in these students who challenge him at a higher
level of academic competence.

In this matter of academic performance, a rehearsal of the problems involved in getting help from the parents of deprived children is perhaps un-
necessary; their inability to aid their children academically or their reluctance
to collaborate with teachers has already been stated or implied. What is interesting is that teachers themselves tend to take it for granted that in matters
of academic performance the parents cannot be of much help. In Hollings-

---

[12]Research Division, National Education Association, *Salary Schedules for Classroom Teachers, 1966–67*, Public-School Salaries Series Research Report 1966-R17
(Washington: National Education Assn., 1966), p. 5.

head's school, for instance, middle-class parents were often consulted on the work of their children (and far less often on questions of discipline), but lower-class parents were drawn into conferences far less frequently for academic reasons than for reasons of discipline and punishment, even though the children were obviously doing very poorly scholastically. In general, as research in the Detroit inner city has shown, teachers take the dimmest view of deprived parents, accusing them of the following variety of traits, none of them conducive to scholarship:[13]

1. They do not encourage high academic achievement, even work against it.
2. They scorn teachers.
3. They do not attend school organization meetings such as the PTA.
4. They cannot provide school community leadership when given tasks to perform.
5. They are cruel to their children and ignorant of child development.
6. They are difficult to deal with, unreasonable, and sometimes drunk and violent.

Naturally if deprived parents sense that teachers have these attitudes toward them, the result is inevitably greater apathy and greater estrangement from the school.

THE AIMS AND FUNCTIONS OF PUBLIC EDUCATION

At one time or another various people have listed the aims of public education. As long ago as 1927, Leonard V. Koos wrote down four principal things that students should achieve upon graduation: (1) civic, social, and moral responsibility, (2) recreational and esthetic participation and appreciation, (3) occupational efficiency, including academic preparation for the college-bound, and (4) physical efficiency.[14] Such aims differ very little from those in a more recent listing by another educator; only the wording and flavor are different: (1) *humanistic education*, to "help the child comprehend his experience and find meaning in life," (2) *citizenship education*, to develop "active, aware citizens who will work devotedly for [society's] improvement," and (3) *intellectual education*, to have the child "acquire the analytic ideas and problem-solving tools that are developed by scholars."[15] To these broad, generalized aims, of course, we often find added the specific aims of acquiring the fundamentals of reading, writing, and arithmetic and the fundamentals of health and science.

---

[13]Research Committee of the Coordinating Council on Human Relations, Detroit (see footnote 2).

[14]Leonard V. Koos, *The American Secondary School* (Boston: Ginn, 1927), Chap. 5.

[15]Bruce R. Joyce, *Strategies for Elementary Social Science Education* (Chicago: Science Research Associates, 1965), p. 3.

Anyone who has studied the deprived is immediately struck by the middle-class orientation of lists of this sort. They come right out of the value patterns of middle-class people with their appreciation of academic education, their orientation toward careers and occupations, their interest in enriching experiences in recreation and leisure activities, and their desire for respectable civic responsibility. The only items that would seem to have any immediate interest for the deprived would be the fundamentals — the three R's and health and science. And even these can be uninteresting abstractions if they are treated as ends in themselves rather than as skills necessary for preserving one's health and getting a job, the only objectives really comprehensible to the deprived youth.

Consider the teaching of health, for example. The emphasis is not pragmatic, awarding the best grades to students who strive to adopt the recommended health practices; it is instead academic or abstract, awarding the best grades to those who can summon up knowledge about the nomenclature and functions of bodily organs or about the varieties of vitamins and minerals in foods. Such an emphasis may be entirely proper for the middle-class student who comes to school healthy and bounding with the energy from a good diet and who has been influenced to have some measure of intellectual curiosity. Such an emphasis, however, may seem quite meaningless to the more practical-minded, anti-intellectual student from deprived neighborhoods.

The deprived youngster's attitude is much more utilitarian. Education is not understood "as an opportunity for the development of self-expression, self-realization, growth, and the like."[16] Education, instead, is viewed as a means of acquiring a secure job (and security in general) — often in governmental agencies that open their doors more readily to him provided he has the literacy and ability to pass civil service examinations. To be educated is to be prepared for the examinations leading into the coveted positions of fireman, postal clerk, hospital orderly. To be educated is to be vocationally trained and acceptably literate. His interest is not in what we consider the academic aspect of education.

The difference between "academic" and "vocational" education may not seem so disparate, however, if one considers their aims. Insofar as academic work can represent preparation for a college education, which in turn develops a person for learned professions — law, medicine, engineering, finance, teaching, research, and so forth — it can be considered a form of occupational training. In providing placement services for their seniors and graduates, colleges actually recognize this transition or connection between full-time schooling and full-time jobs. As James B. Conant has noted, "While the universities or colleges do not accept responsibility for the placement of

---

[16]Riessman, p. 12.

their graduates, many, if not all, spend time and money in helping the young man or woman to find a job. In many cases the subsequent career is followed with interest, and assistance is provided in re-employment."[17] Of course, ideally a college education develops the person as well as the worker, but the aspect of job training is certainly not negligible.

When we turn to the culturally deprived, we find that their aims are not fundamentally different. They want education for a job, but, as we said in the preceding chapter, their aspirations are for entry into the Good Life, not for the sophisticated embellishments that middle-class youth with a living knowledge of the Good Life can understand and realistically hope for. Deprived youth therefore want an education that clearly in their own minds prepares them for the jobs within their ken. They want to be able to see that between their work in school and their work on the job there is a perceivable transition, a clear connection. For this reason, they prefer what we call vocational training. If we reduce things to a common denominator, we can recognize that both middle- and lower-class youth define education as a preparation for the Good Life, but they simply have different conceptions of the careers, and thus the education, that provide it.

The principle of vocational training was recognized and implemented many years ago with the development of technical schools for youth planning not to enter college but to enter trades upon graduation. In large cities such schools were reasonably effective, and insofar as they involved learning activities of a physical nature that lower-class youth appreciated, they exercised some holding power on these youth. Unquestionably, the how-to-do-it courses in these schools did help many of them toward a trade that provided a future for themselves and their families.

The great problem was expense. To provide the necessary machines and equipment — particularly if they were to be constantly renewed and kept current with the rapidly changing technology of modern society — required a great expenditure per pupil. The materials for the academic student are not nearly so costly as those for the technical student. Thus, politics being what they are, equipment was left to become out of date; and in smaller schools in rural areas and small towns, there could never be even the initial expenditures for a wide variety of facilities for carpentry, farming, plumbing, electrical work, auto mechanics, and so forth. Many small schools might afford facilities for one or another activity — for carpentry or electrical work, for instance — but usually not for all.

Technical training for girls was generally more successful than that for boys — for the very reasons of financial capability. Business or commercial courses in bookkeeping, filing, stenography, and the like are not expensive

---

[17]James B. Conant, *Slums and Suburbs* (New York: McGraw-Hill, 1961), p. 40.

to offer. Even typewriters, though initially expensive, can be depreciated over the years and involve enough students to keep the cost per pupil low. Business courses, it goes without saying, represent the kind of education that the culturally deprived can find meaningful and relevant.

Putting aside for the moment the real problem of financial capabilities, we might perhaps see a greater problem in the nonvocational portion of the students' education. Changes in their vocational training may not have been accompanied by necessary changes in their academic work in reading, writing, arithmetic, and so forth. As behaviorally oriented educators have recently insisted, education, like any other institution, should be a system of interdependent parts, and if we revise one part we must adjust others, for they interact and influence one another.[18] Certainly many educators feel that academic programs and materials have not in the past been readjusted for deprived students in the same fashion as vocational courses have. Thus there has been a recent spate of materials written specifically for the deprived under such names as slow-learner materials and integrated textbooks.

One such attempt at adapting academic work to the needs and experiences of deprived children has been undertaken by Gerald Weinstein, curriculum coordinator of the Madison Area Project in Syracuse, New York. One report describes his method as follows:[19]

> . . . Rather than using a nineteenth-century poem from a standard school anthology, he used one full of current "hip" jargon by Negro author Langston Hughes as a point of departure for discussion. The students, in sharp contrast to their previously apathetic attitude, now were alive, animated, and involved, since this was on their "turf." For some of them it may have been the first time in their school experience that they could exhibit knowledge and have some sense of success and accomplishment. . . . The enthusiasm of that class session led the students into more of Hughes's poetry. Later they moved into other kinds of literature in more conventional language.

Favorable reports of this kind are numerous, but we are still in a period of experimentation that has not yielded definitive answers to how we can effectively reach the culturally deprived in various situations. We might close this chapter with a note of warning from another educator:[20]

---

[18]See Francis A. J. Ianni, *Culture, System, and Behavior: The Behavioral Sciences and Education* (Chicago: Science Research Associates, 1967).

[19]Frank Riessman and Arlene Hannah, "Teachers of the Poor," *PTA Magazine,* LIX (November 1964), 14.

[20]From "Teachers of the Culturally Disadvantaged" by Bruce R. Joyce, as it appeared in *Teaching the Culturally Disadvantaged Pupil,* 1965, edited by John M. Beck and Richard W. Saxe (Springfield, Ill.: Charles C Thomas, 1965).

The teacher for the inner city must not think to himself: "The reason they don't learn to read is because the readers deal with things outside their experience. The readers show ivy-covered cottages and dogs and cats and jolly grandmothers in the country. That stuff doesn't make sense to the slum child." While I personally have little brief with the content of many reading books, the logic in the quotation just made is about as valid as the argument that children will not like nursery stories about kings and dragons because they have not encountered them in their daily life.

What I am trying to say, of course, is that the teacher of the culturally disadvantaged has to enter teaching with a deep sense of our ignorance about inner-city children and how to treat them. He has to beware of shibboleths and treat with circumspection the doctrines of even the most successful teacher or the most careful psychologist. *This is no time for dogma.* Any beginning teacher in the slums who thinks he has the answers and who tries to teach in accord with the prescribed answers will come to grief very shortly.

Suggested Readings

BLOOM, S. B.; DAVIS, A.; and HESS, R. *Compensatory Education for Cultural Deprivation.* New York: Holt, Rinehart & Winston, 1965.

HAVIGHURST, ROBERT J., and NEUGARTEN, B. L. *Society and Education.* Boston: Allyn & Bacon, 1962.

JOHN, VERA P. "The Intellectual Development of Slum Children: Some Preliminary Findings," *American Journal of Orthopsychiatry,* XXXIII (October 1963), 813–22.

RIVLIN, HARRY N. *Teachers for Our Big City Schools.* New York: Anti-Defamation League of B'nai B'rith, 1964.

SCHORR, L. A. *Poor Kids: A Report on Children in Poverty.* New York: Basic Books, 1966.

SCHREIBER, D. (ed.). *The School Dropout.* Washington: National Education Assn., 1964.

Chapter Five: GUIDELINES FOR A TEACHING METHODOLOGY

Clearly neither the school nor the teacher can be expected to compensate for the many deficiencies that the disadvantaged youngster brings with him to school. The school cannot be expected to erase memories of bitterness and despair. The teacher cannot take the place of a father or mother, on either a full- or a part-time basis. The school system cannot provide all the medical and dental care essential to good health. It would be naive to believe that through the educational process alone we shall establish a social system that will lead to the elimination of poverty. On the contrary, the school is but one social institution within a complex of institutions that constitute our society and our way of life.

The fact that poverty exists in this country, however, added to the fact that this nation has yet to create adequate institutions to deal with the educational needs of the poor, is indicative of a national failure. If every agency and institution responsible for socializing the young had done its job, there would be no need for programs of intervention such as the Job Corps, the

Neighborhood Youth Corps, Operation Head Start, and various local educational projects. The need for such programs reflects this nation's total inability to cope with a primary and vital task — the preparation of the young for taking on responsible and productive adult roles.

There is, no doubt, much that our schools can and must do in order to enhance the status of poor youth. What the school and the teacher must do — during that period of time in which they deal with the children — is to provide the type of educational climate that will maximize the learning and retention of skills essential for life in a highly complex society. The teacher who works with the poor must recognize that these children lack essential resources that are available to most middle-class youth. They are frequently deprived of financial, material, parental, and social supports. They have limited access to adults who can intervene on their behalf. Their out-of-school life is not filled with opportunities for intellectual exploration. On the other hand, we should not assume, as we have been inclined to assume, that poor youth are a totally different breed in need of a totally different type of educational program. Education of the poor does not necessitate the rediscovery of the wheel.

So concentrated have our recent efforts been on the problem of the disadvantaged that we have failed to utilize our limited knowledge of learning already acquired through the study of other segments of the population. In other words, we have treated this group of poor youth as a body for which a whole new set of pedagogical techniques and curricula would have to be developed if they were, in fact, to go through our educational system. Without valid reason, we have tended to abandon our understandings and insights, painfully acquired, of children's behavior, of the social systems of schools, and of the needs of children, and to start all over again.

This is not to imply that there is no need for a clear identification of the problem or an outline of the characteristics of the population we seek to help. The point is that we have already reached the initial stage of the art. It is safe to say we know at least the general dimensions of the problem.

Admittedly, any solution proposed at this time has only a small probability of being totally correct. The problem, however, is of such magnitude that initial propositions toward solutions are mandatory.

What follows here are some general propositions on the education of deprived youth. Although these are directed primarily to persons who work with adolescents, we believe that the method may also apply to those who teach younger children.[1]

---

[1]The model presented in the following pages was developed by one of the authors, David Gottlieb, in cooperation with Professor Louis Guttman of the Hebrew University of Israel and has been implemented in a number of Job Corps centers. The evaluation data on the effectiveness of the technique were collected and analyzed by members of the Job Corps Evaluation Branch.

THE GOALS OF DEPRIVED YOUTH

Basically, youth behave in much the same way anywhere — that is, in any sociocultural context and no matter what their background. Adolescents will become oriented to or involved with those whom they perceive to have the desire and ability to help them attain their goals. Thus socialization involves three interrelated conditions:

1. The adolescent must perceive *congruence* between his goals and the goals of his teacher or socializer.
2. The adolescent must perceive that his socializer has the *desire* to help him attain his goals.
3. The adolescent must perceive that his socializer has the *ability* to help him attain his goals.

Only when these three conditions are met can there be maximum involvement between student and teacher, student and guidance counselor, or student and peer — or, for that matter, between any child and any referent.

As for goals, there is no question but that every youth does have them, no matter how vague they may seem. Adults may disagree with his goals at any given time, but his world exists as he sees it and not always as we would like him to see it. Where youngsters of different backgrounds do part company is in the articulation of these goals. As we have said repeatedly, whereas the middle-class youth knows rather clearly what constitutes the Good Life — higher education, professional careers, homes, clothes, travel, and so forth — the lower-class youth has only a dim awareness of what can be had in this world and how to get it. He knows only the exterior of the Good Life, and his wants thus remain rather elemental (from the middle-class point of view). As an illustration, the goal of having nice clothes would be of less immediate importance to a child with an abundance of clothes than it would be to the youngster without shoes. The goal of achieving an A on an examination would more likely be held by a student who had received a B on his midterm than by one who had failed the same examination.

In the same vein, a student whose parents are educated and who looks forward to college will at least put up with the work required of him in high school and may even see some value in studying history or literature or advanced mathematics. A student who seeks merely entry into the Good Life by getting a good steady job as farmer, mechanic, or postal clerk, however, is not likely to see much relevance in studying history, literature, or advanced mathematics. One of his most important motivations for dropping out of school, in fact, is his recognition — and our frequent failure to recognize — that much of what goes on in school is of little practical value to him. In the past we have expected him to adjust his goals to ours, when in reality we ought to readjust our approach to meet his needs and his realistic aspirations. As we said at the beginning of this chapter, education cannot be considered a panacea that will eradicate all the disadvantages already instilled in the youngster upon entering school and miraculously raise him to the upper-middle class with all its understanding and appreciation of the finer aspects of the Good Life.

That poor youth do insist that their goals and the goals expected of them by teachers are incongruent is evidenced by the results of questionnaires presented to Job Corpsmen. Only 14 percent thought there was a high degree of congruence; 49 percent saw only moderate or infrequent agreement between them and their teachers. About 37 percent of the total saw no agreement or almost no agreement whatsoever. No wonder, then, that these youth feel so alienated and see no reason for getting very much involved in classroom activities. Unaware of the possible benefits of continuing their education just for the sake of a diploma, they may have an immediate desire for something better than their current condition, seeking something away from school, perhaps in any job that will earn them money quick, give them some status, and free them somehow from the despair of their paltry existence.

Before leaving this question of goal congruence, we maybe should say a word about the 14 percent who did feel that they and their teachers were in tune. Perhaps among them we find those few who somehow acquire imagination, intellectual curiosity, and understanding despite the barren nature of their environment. They are no doubt the ones who find their way to become teachers, businessmen, and other professionals of higher status. We mentioned such teachers in the preceding chapter.[2] All that this proves, however, is that there are exceptions and that we must not routinely stereotype a student solely on the basis of his background. The exceptions do not disprove the rule that perhaps 86 out of 100 deprived youngsters generally find sophisticated middle-class goals incomprehensible or unrealistic.

THE DESIRE AND ABILITY TO HELP DEPRIVED YOUTH

In addition to judging whether the teacher's goals match his own, the student evaluates his teacher on both ability and desire to help him attain his goals. Only those who meet the test favorably will get the student interested and involved.

A deprived youngster is no more unrealistic than any other human being. He knows he has few human resources to rely on. Unlike the middle-class youth, he does not have parents able to help him upward, and he knows it. This is not to say that his parents — if he has parents — do not care or lack

---

[2] See pp. 55–57.

the desire to help him; they may indeed wish him good. (Foster parents or other guardians, admittedly, may not always care.) This does mean, however, that he does not consider his parents to be persons who have the social, financial, or political skills to help. If he is to get any help, he must turn to people outside the immediate family and, unlike his middle-class peer, become dependent on such people whether he likes it or not. Naturally, if he fails to find these other people, complete resignation or defeatism may set in, turning him into a Clark, Pearl, Ruth, or other drifter of the type described earlier.[3]

When we consider their need for outside help, it is saddening to see the way in which most deprived adolescents view their teachers. Although middle-class youngsters themselves scarcely consider all their teachers able and willing to the point of perfection, deprived youth are apt to view them as almost completely alien. Whether we elicit the opinions of rich or poor, teachers do not fare too well, but the poor feel far more deprived in this respect — and in fact are generally deprived of understanding and able teachers.

Among the deprived, Negro youngsters are especially prone to view the world as either alien or unhelpful. Although they do feel that their Negro teachers desire to help them — far more so than their white teachers — they join with their white peers in considering white teachers to be generally possessed of greater ability. In general, Negro as well as white youth have tended to accept the cliché that in cognitive areas Negroes are less able than whites; undoubtedly this negative self-concept proceeds from years of discrimination and segregation which even the Supreme Court described in the historic desegregation case, *Brown v. Board of Education* (1954): "To separate them from others of similar age and qualifications solely because of their race generates a feeling of inferiority as to their status in the community that may affect their hearts and minds in a way unlikely ever to be undone."[4]

Furthermore, that Negro youth generally consider their white teachers unwilling to help probably derives from the same years and years of mutual distrust. Such distrust is currently reinforced when Negro students see that when the racial composition of a school changes from white to Negro, the exodus of white teachers begins. Negro students are not unaware that, given

---

[3]See pp. 20–28.

[4]Of further interest are the research findings of Irwin Katz, who has listed three psychological conditions that tend to deprive Negro students of success in integrated schools where the majority whites are generally discriminatory: "*Low probability of success* — where there is marked discrepancy in the educational standards of Negro and white schools, or where feelings of inferiority are acquired by Negro children outside the school, minority-group newcomers in integrated classrooms are likely to have a low expectancy of academic success; consequently, their achievement motivation should be low. *Social threat* — given the prestige and power of the white majority group, rejection of Negro students by white classmates or teachers should tend to

their choice, teachers prefer a suburban school where few, if any, Negroes are found. As one student in an inner-city school expressed it:

> We had this social science teacher, and she was always telling us how it used to be. She would tell us that teaching used to be a challenge. Her students were interested in their studies, and most of them went on to college. She was always telling us how all that had changed — that we just don't appreciate how important education is and how exciting it could be. She kept on like that all the time. One day she said she was going to a new school where she could teach again. A whole bunch of the white teachers have left because they don't want to be in this school.

A METHODOLOGY FOR INDUCING THE STUDENT'S INVOLVEMENT

Any student, deprived or otherwise, will be motivated to learn only if he perceives that his teachers and counselors are able and willing to give him at least three kinds of support. They must give him *instrumental aid*, convincing him that what he is doing from day to day is marked by progress, both short-term and long-range in view of his ultimate goals. They must give him *cognitive aid*, providing him with "maps" of ways to do things that will show him how he can accomplish what he individually wants to accomplish; this requires giving him information, illustrations, and clarifications and tailoring various means to his particular needs and objectives. They must finally give him *affective aid*, showing him that they do care and that they are sincerely interested in his ideas and problems. If the student receives these various aids, he himself has a better chance of developing instrumentally, cognitively, and affectively — acquiring the ability to evaluate his own progress, use various skills, and take an interest in learning. The overall result hopefully will be to usher him into the Good Life and achieve the ultimate goals of education, which are employment, utilization of social institutions, utilization of leisure-time resources, social and political involvement, and physical and mental health. The chart on page 72 illustrates the full train of events.

---

elicit emotional responses (fear, anger, and humiliation) that are detrimental to intellectual functioning. *Failure threat* — when academic failure entails disapproval by significant others (parents, teachers, and perhaps also classmates), low expectancy of success should elicit emotional responses that are detrimental to performance.

"On the other hand," says Katz, "acceptance of Negroes by white peers and adults should have a *social facilitation* effect upon their ability to learn, by motivating them to adhere to white standards of academic performance; anticipation that high performance will win white approval should endow scholastic success with *high-incentive value*." From "Review of Evidence Relating to Effects of Desegregation on the Intellectual Performance of Negroes," *American Psychologist*, XIX (June 1964), 396.

The more the school staff offers the student in the way of

Instrumental Aid
- Continual indications of his progress
- Long-range prospects of reward as a result of his progress

Cognitive Aid
- Information about the means for attaining his goals
- Illustrations of the means for attaining his goals
- Clarification about the means for attaining his goals
- Individual tailoring of the means for attaining his goals

Affective Aid
- Active concern for his ideas
- Active concern for his problems

The more the student will perceive the staff as willing and able to help him as an individual, and the more the school will achieve its goals of promoting the student's

Instrumental Development
- Ability to see and measure his own progress

Cognitive Development
- Achievement of technical skills

Affective Development
- Desire to learn

And the more the student will achieve the ultimate aims of education, which are

- Employment
- Utilization of social institutions
- Utilization of leisure-time resources
- Social and political involvement
- Physical and mental health

How this methodology works in practice is illustrated by the Job Corps Advisory System, which has been adopted in a few centers throughout the country. Upon entering a center, a young person is immediately assigned to a corpsman adviser, who can be any member of the permanent staff — cook, teacher, work leader, or counselor — and whose role is to provide the instrumental, cognitive, and affective aid associated with the corpsman's progress. He plays an important part in the lives of the corpsmen in his care. He helps them define and choose their occupational goals. He keeps track of each one's progress in work and education. And he holds regularly scheduled conferences with each corpsman, during which, among other things, the corpsman's progress is discussed and recorded. Thus counseled, the student can see his own progress in every phase of the total program. In order to accomplish this rapport and full understanding, of course, the adviser has a fairly simple but precise system of receiving up-to-date reports from various staffers throughout the center and recording the results not only in the trainee's individual portfolio but also on a "Summary Progress Board" displayed for all to see. The rationale for the publicity is partly to involve all corpsmen in the responsibility of helping one another and partly to reward publicly any gains and promotions merited by individual trainees. Promotions, in fact, are accompanied by brief, but visible, award ceremonies.

The adviser's initial task is naturally to help an incoming trainee decide on his vocational goals. Being only vaguely aware of the choices open to him and the interests, personality traits, and talents required in different occupations, the trainee needs some definite guidance. The Job Chart shown on page 74 is used by the adviser to try to guide every trainee into realistic goals. If the student recognizes that he has only a marginal talent in "public relations," for instance, he perhaps should be guided away from such jobs as those performed by waiters or service station attendants. Resort to the Job Chart is not rigid; it serves only as a guide. But it does give both the adviser and the trainee a rough idea of the possible areas to move into, of deficiencies to be overcome, and of skills to be acquired.

The adviser and the corpsman then together develop a plan of schooling, which specifies not only the goals, long-range and intermediate, but also the means of reaching the goals. The plan is thus tailored to the individual's needs. Thereafter the adviser continually provides information and further clarifications, retailoring the means or courses of instruction whenever this seems necessary.

One of the most valuable ingredients of the adviser-corpsman relationship is the openness of discussion, the free give-and-take of opinions, feelings, and information during the regular conferences. Customarily in schools, deprived students get only random, if any, opportunities to express their grievances or air their difficulties. They generally believe, often correctly, that teachers do not care about them or that speaking one's sentiments only draws penalties. The corpsman adviser, on the other hand, is encourged to listen to what the student thinks and feels — and not only listen but take immediate action that will pointedly show his desire to help and also his ability to bring about changes on the student's behalf. Armed with the belief that his adviser and the rest of the staff have indeed the desire and ability to help him, the student inevitably puts in much greater effort and makes much better progress toward his goals — instrumentally, cognitively, and affectively. He begins to devise and evaluate ways of measuring or understanding his progress. He begins to master the necessary technical skills. And he develops a strong desire to achieve and learn.

In those Job Corps centers using the Advisory System, the results have been dramatic and positive. Compared with their peers in other centers,

Key: ■ high level skill   ▨ medium level skill   ⊡ low level skill   JOB CHART

Handbook for Corpsman Advisors, Job Corps Conservation Centers, A Xerox Education Division Program (Copyright © 1966, Basic Systems, Inc. All Rights Reserved).

youth under the Advisory System have tended more often to remain in the Job Corps until completion of their training and, most significantly, have tended toward greater achievements. Those who had dropped out of public school with third-grade reading and mathematics skills, for instance, have been mastering about two additional grade levels every four months. Their "antisocial" behavior, moreover, has tended to ameliorate, once they have known that they can freely speak their piece and get things off their chest, under the guidance of an understanding adviser.

The motivations and aspirations of these youth have risen markedly. For many, feelings of success, in even the slightest degree, have brought about changes in their self-concepts. Where before they had expressed doubts about their ability to master the simplest of tasks, they have now appeared willing at least to chance more complex problems. Where initially they had expressed a desire for learning fairly fundamental job skills, they have now aspired to higher levels of occupational training.

Perhaps most surprising to everyone in the Job Corps has been the number of corpsmen who have been expressing a desire to return to school in order to complete their formal education — surprising because so many of these young people had left school either as dropouts, throw-outs, or push-outs with mixed feelings of relief and bitterness. The feeling of relief had resulted from being able to break out of a setting that they had seen as confining and hostile. The feeling of bitterness had resulted because, although they had made every effort to conform and to meet imposed expectations, they had in fact been rejected by the educational system. Evidently this new form of learning, the Job Corps Advisory System, which incorporates a close and continuous relationship between student and adult, has led some of these youngsters to try the traditional system once again.

Adapted to local conditions, this educational model introduced by the Job Corps should work among various groups of deprived youth. Perhaps the most important element is making the students aware that there are valid reasons for becoming involved in learning and that there are adults both desirous and able to assist them in learning skills and behaviors necessary for the employment they seek and for their adjustment to our complex society. If the social climate of the school seems more responsive to their needs and feelings, their probability of success is heightened.

As we said earlier, there is nothing particularly new in this theory of learning. It has long been applied to middle-class children. But it has been poorly applied — if applied at all — to children of poverty.

The conditions of poverty and deprivation described in this volume are not unique to any one group of students or any single type of school. Nor is the social climate we have described favorable only to certain children or certain classrooms. On the contrary, an educational approach involving interested and able adults will have at least an even chance of captivating the student's attention, his energy, and his respect, so that he can have the interest, the motivation, and the confidence to be educated.

Suggested Readings

BECKER, HOWARD S. "Social Class and Teacher-Pupil Relationships," pp. 273–85 in *Education and the Social Order*, eds. BLAIN E. MERCER and EDWIN R. CARR. New York: Holt, Rinehart & Winston, 1957. Reprinted from "Social-Class Variations in the Teacher-Pupil Relationship," *Journal of Educational Sociology*, XXV (April 1952), 451–65.

CHANDLER, B. J.; STILES, LINDLEY J.; and KITSUSEY, JOHN I. (eds.). *Education in Urban Society*. New York: Dodd, Mead, 1962.

CLARK, BURTON R. *Educating the Expert Society*. San Francisco: Chandler, 1962.

COLEMAN, JAMES S., AND OTHERS. *Equality of Educational Opportunity*. Washington: Department of Health, Education, and Welfare, 1966.

GOSLIN, DAVID A. *The School in Contemporary Society*. Glenview, Ill.: Scott, Foresman, 1965.